INTEGRITY

Integrity

Doing the Right Thing
for the Right Reason

BARBARA KILLINGER, Ph.D.

McGill-Queen's University Press
Montreal & Kingston • London • Ithaca

ISBN 978-0-7735-3287-8

Legal deposit third quarter 2007
Bibliothèque nationale du Québec

Printed in Canada on acid-free paper that is 100% ancient forest
free (100% post-consumer recycled), processed chlorine free

McGill-Queen's University Press acknowledges the support of the
Canada Council for the Arts for our publishing program. We also
acknowledge the financial support of the Government of Canada
through the Book Publishing Industry Development Program
(BPIDP) for our publishing activities.

Library and Archives Canada Cataloguing in Publication

Killinger, Barbara
    Integrity: doing the right thing for the right reason / Barbara
Killinger.

Includes bibliographical references and index.
ISBN 978-0-7735-3287-8

1. Integrity. I. Title.

BJ1533.I58K54 2007   179'.9   C2007-902836-5

Lyrics quoted on page 178–9 are taken from Into the Woods, music
and lyrics by STEPHEN SONDHEIM and JAMES LAPINE, © 1988 RILTING
MUSIC, INC. All rights administered by WB MUSIC CORP. All rights
reserved. Used by permission of ALFRED PUBLISHING CO., INC.

Typeset by Jay Tee Graphics Ltd. in 10.5/13 New Baskerville

In memory of our much loved parents, Eva and Cuyler Henderson,
who were inspirational role models for integrity,
unconditional love, and compassion

Contents

Acknowledgments

I wish to thank my clients and others who generously agreed to share their views on integrity, as well as their stories of those people in their lives who do possess this most precious trait.

The Honourable Coulter A. Osborne, Integrity Commissioner of Ontario, graciously agreed to read my manuscript and offered helpful comments. As always, I am most grateful to my children, who have listened and supported me in my writing career.

Thanks go to Philip Cercone, editors Maureen Garvie and Joan McGilvray, and others at McGill-Queen's University Press who guided this book through the production process and beyond.

Special thanks to Stephen Sondheim for granting his permission to quote from the lyrics to his wonderful musical, *Into the Woods*.

Names and situational details in the text have been changed to protect privacy.

INTEGRITY

Doing the Right Thing
for the Right Reason

Introduction

Morality and ethics remain popular topics, yet relatively little has been written on integrity.

A psychological approach to this subject makes sense, because integrity is an internal state of being that guides us towards making morally wise choices. In contrast, morality and ethics are externally imposed values consensually acknowledged by societal standards to be for the common good.

"What got you interested in this subject?" an editor asks. Perhaps a poem written by Charlie Crocker on the occasion of my father's forty-fifth anniversary at the London Life Insurance Company will reveal why integrity has played an influential role in my own life.

Once in a long time, one is privileged to know a man
Who is set apart from the rest
Who is capable, kind and considerate in his dealings with
others.
Who can chide where required, but who does it in such a
manner one is not crushed or made to feel inferior.
Who has the ability to use words which contain just the right
shade of meaning.
Who gives of himself unstintingly to his job.
Who will back you up when you need it.
Who makes you feel you and the work you do are important.
Whose personal qualities and ideals are above reproach.
Whose standard of morals and ethics are high.
Who cherishes his family and his Church.
Who does not betray a confidence or deprecate other people.

Who will take the time to write you a personal note to give you a
lift when you feel down.
Who does the many little things that make you appreciate how
big a man he really is.
I know such a man.
His name is Cuyler Henderson – a man I am proud to call both
my boss and friend.

As a pioneer in the study of workaholism, I discovered that there
were two crucial turning points in the predictable breakdown syndrome that this dangerous addiction follows: the inevitable but
tragic loss of feeling, and the subsequent moral loss of integrity. My
book *Workaholics: The Respectable Addicts* presented a clinical and
theoretical study of workaholism and its negative effects on the
individual, both at home and in the work setting. *The Balancing Act:
Rediscovering Your Feelings* offered practical solutions to help workaholics restore their inner balance through a problem-solving
process I call "Internalizing."

My present concern is the moral development of integrity, the
reasons and ways in which it is lost, and methods of safeguarding it.
Swiss psychologist Carl Jung's theories of psychological type and his
concepts of the positive and negative Shadow traits and the Inferior
function have all proven to be invaluable in this task of formulating
a theoretical backdrop for how the dark side of the personality can
sabotage integrity.

Although my focus here is on personal integrity, we are now seeing widespread concern about its survival at a societal level, and
rightly so. We live in an increasingly valueless society where success
is measured primarily by status, prestige, and power. Materialism
and its partner, consumerism, nurture the evils of greed, envy, lust,
and shame – all enemies of integrity. Recent reports of outrageous
acts of corporate fraud have sent shock waves of alarm around the
world. Disillusioned and gravely insecure, we ask the $64 question,
"What's gone wrong?"

Narcissism is the antithesis of integrity. Our era, which Christopher
Lasch has called the Age of Narcissism, is suffering from the fallout
of the Enlightenment and the rise of individualism, which champions the rights of the individual over the welfare of the state and its
citizens. Solid values that consider the common good have
declined in this impersonal, fast-track, technological world. Collec-

tively, these seductive forces relegate feeling values to an after-thought. In his prophetic wisdom, Jung warned that unless the world soon embraced the feminine principle by adopting feeling values, it was doomed to self-destruction.

Workaholism is increasingly prevalent worldwide, yet not enough people realize that workaholics gradually become emotionally crippled and addicted to power and control in their obsessive drive for public recognition and success. Profound personality changes occur when all one's energy is poured into building a persona that broadcasts success. Feelings grow numb and empathy disappears. The capacity to be sensitive, fair, and compassionate is sacrificed as the traits of honesty, self-control, and duty are replaced by gross manipulation, lies, broken promises, and cruel insensitivity.

Integrity suffers greatly when "whatever works" is seen as acceptable, and what doesn't ceases to inform judgment. The "big picture" is eclipsed as myopic, short-term, bottom-line thinking takes charge.

As the glory days of the 1980s gave way to the hard economic times of the 1990s, mergers, corporate takeovers, and massive lay-offs meant more work for less staff. Some earnest types were "Peter Principled" – promoted to jobs that were well beyond their level of expertise. Those who remained in the workforce sometimes suffered pangs of guilt, but had to work harder and smarter to keep their own jobs. The resultant climate of fear and acute stress has created an unhealthy work environment that does not encourage integrity.

This book is about understanding integrity and how ordinary people behave when confronted with moral and ethical issues. The views of people I interviewed illuminate many of the ideas presented here.

Part 1 introduces and defines integrity, and explains the development of the key personality traits considered necessary to build character and a healthy conscience. A philosophical overview lays the groundwork for understanding why narcissism is so prevalent today and how it corrupts integrity.

Part 2 looks at how integrity is lost. Unhealthy coping mechanisms fostered by dysfunctional family rules and patterns damage our character, as do the other enemies of integrity – alienation, secrecy, repression, manipulation, cynicism, and perfectionism. With so many public figures falling from grace, it is increasingly difficult for parents to teach the values of integrity to their children.

I take a Jungian approach to show why compulsive obsessions play a central role in leading a person towards moral chaos. Workaholism is a special case of obsession that is complicated by the addiction to power and control. Integrity is undermined whenever we exhibit the dark personality traits of arrogance and intolerance, shame and seduction, anger and resentment, greed and sloth. I single out dishonesty and wilful behaviour for special attention.

In part 3 I suggest a number of things we can do that will help improve our present level of integrity.

Firstly, we can free ourselves from temptation by transforming our weaknesses into strengths. To do so, we need to consciously acknowledge the dark Shadow side of our personality. Jung's theory of type helps identify the dangerous Inferior function in each of us – the trait most likely to undermine our integrity.

Secondly, we can strengthen our integrity by making a conscious decision to follow an "understanding path" rather than a judgmental one. The problem-solving technique of Internalizing can help the reader develop an inner core of values. This proactive process encourages us to be more personally responsible for our own reactions and subsequent actions.

Lastly, if we are parents, we can be better role models for our children by striving for personal "wholeness." We can diligently guide them toward sound beliefs and values and a healthy respect for rules, regulations, and laws. In the workplace we have a further chance to set an example, to put into practice the values we've chosen to live by.

Integrity should be integrated into our character, beyond choice. This means honouring our highest values and resisting temptation, striving for a more balanced psyche, and being more appreciative of what we already have. Integrity requires us to perform compassionate acts. By serving and helping others, we ourselves become more fully human.

An acquaintance recently told me that his father always did the right thing, but clearly it was often for the wrong reason. He then raised a question worth thinking about as we explore the true meaning of integrity: Did his father have integrity?

PART ONE

What Is Integrity and How Does It Develop?

1

Integrity in a Dishonest World

Telling the truth about the terrible struggle of the human soul is surely a very elementary part of the ethics of honesty.

G.K. Chesterton, *All Things Considered*

THE PUBLIC AND PRIVATE FACES OF INTEGRITY

How do we really know if someone has integrity?

There's much trauma and angst involved when integrity is lost, yet we rarely hear first hand about the sufferings of those who have experienced this personal tragedy. Before going on to explore the meaning and importance of integrity, let's listen to the poignant private reflections of one individual. You may know someone like him.

LOST

Somewhere along the path I've trod
I've lost my sense of Self, of God
I've lost the sense of who I am
I'm empty now; a shell, a sham

I vainly search my past to see
The hope filled child that once was me
Some glimpse that lets me feel again
The joy and innocence of then

What are the roots of my despair?
What terror overtook me there?
Why have I hid from he who's me?
What do I fear to know, to see?

Oh what a vile thing must I be?
In darkness hid lest someone see
Doomed from prison walls to stare
At life in which I cannot share

Please take my hand, help me reveal
Just who I am and what I feel
Lead me back from the abyss
Life cannot go on like this.

Stephen, the writer of this heartbreaking poem, is a much-admired businessman with a seemingly flawless public persona. This driven and energetic chief executive officer built his pharmaceutical company into an industry giant in less than fifteen years. Known for his persuasive and chivalrous charm, Stephen is an excellent motivational speaker who easily inspires his sales staff to outperform last year's quotas. He has become well known and highly respected in the community for his humanitarian work and is justly proud of a service citation he received from the local Rotary Club several years ago.

About six months ago the fire suddenly seemed to go out of Stephen. He began to appear grey and drawn and was experiencing fierce temper tantrums that frightened both his wife and their children. His doctor sent Stephen to see me to investigate why he might be suffering from severe panic attacks and troublesome insomnia.

The above poem was born out of a chance remark Stephen made, and my subsequent challenge for self-confrontation.

"I write poetry sometimes," he mentions sheepishly during a Gestalt exercise intended to help him explore who he *is*, separate from what he *does*. Gestalt therapy techniques make use of chairs to differentiate separate parts of one's personality that are in conflict, so that later integration can take place. Mature and balanced individuals embrace both the negative and positive aspects of their character so that their weaknesses can be transformed.

Stephen, his back to me, faces three chairs set out in a circle in the middle of the office. He sits tongue-tied in the chair that represents his "Positive Feeling" side. Obviously distraught, he turns, his face registering alarm. His speechlessness astounds him.

He has just been asked to try to comfort his "Negative Feeling" side in the chair where he's re-experiencing a distressing childhood memory. He suddenly realizes that he has no vocabulary for self-nurturing, nor does he know how to comfort or reassure himself. Instead, he calls himself a "spineless wimp." In his mind the vulnerable martyr-victim side of his personality deserves nothing but abuse, yet it exerts a powerful influence on his character.

Stephen hasn't yet understood that "Negative Feeling" is easily offended, because it tends to take everything that happens personally. Consequently, much of his energy goes into defending himself or justifying his actions. It is so important to him to be seen as strong and successful!

In reality, his life is in shambles. The idealistic dreams of his youth have turned into recurring nightmares. He is living a double life that is profoundly damaging to both his own family and that of his lover. His deep insecurities opened him up to an infatuation with a young administrative assistant who flattered his ego. She adoringly placed Stephen on a pedestal. In her eyes he could do no wrong.

The session ends with our agreeing that Stephen will write a poem describing the function that each of the chairs represented.

Stephen returns the next week. Apparently his "Positive Thinking" only writes business letters! His "Negative Thinking" poem is about a hunter stalking a deer and her fawn through the snow. When the deer, resigned to its fate, turns and faces the hunter, he unexpectedly decides not to shoot – a hopeful sign. Then it is my turn to be speechless as Stephen hesitantly reads "Lost," his heartbreaking poem about his "Negative Feeling" side.

Clearly, Stephen has lacked wisdom in his life choices. Like most people who lose their integrity, he failed to heed the warning signals from his psyche that he was going astray and needed to correct his poor judgment. If not for the frightening panic attacks and sleepless nights, he would have continued on this path of self-destruction and cruel deceit.

The psyche's warning signals can prove invaluable, as a second story illustrates. Addiction to cocaine and alcoholism almost cost British rock star Elton John his career. In Leslie Bennett's *Vanity Fair* article "Still Captain Fantastic," Elton describes himself, prior to entering rehab in 1990, as looking like "Jabba the Hutt." He was suffering severe bouts of depression and was totally out of control, overweight, unkempt, and bloated. "I had lost my sense of values completely. When you do drugs you get lazy and become a slovenly person. And you feel terrible shame. You know you're being a pig; your whole life is a web of lies and deceit. You're always covering your tracks." He thought people didn't know what he was doing, but of course many did. Eventually with the help of friends he recognized that he no longer had the necessary honesty or humility to do something about his problems on his own.

Both Stephen and Elton John fortunately chose to commit themselves to the long hard journey back to health. Conquering personal demons to regain integrity is one thing. Being fortunate enough to re-establish credibility in the community is a challenge of a different magnitude.

A DEFINITION OF INTEGRITY

Integrity is a personal choice, an uncompromising and predictably consistent commitment to honour moral, ethical, spiritual, and artistic values and principles.

Wholeness, a psychological state of internal harmony and consistent moral character, best captures the essence of integrity. The Latin word *integer* from which it is derived means complete, whole, or entire.

In practical terms, the concept of wholeness requires us to see not only the "big picture" but also all the variables involved in a difficult situation. To possess integrity, we must be willing to resist the temptation to focus selectively only on information or aspects that fit our own experience, self-serving needs, or narrowly held views.

There is no integrity in saying one thing and doing another. To be predictable to ourselves and others, our spoken and written words must be consistent with our subsequent choices of action or behaviour. Issues of trust are fundamentally important in our relationships within marriage and the family, as well as in the wider world of commerce where the honouring of contractual agreements is essential to fair trade and profitable dealings.

In the grey areas where right and wrong are not immediately obvious or truth remains elusive, integrity requires us to spend a serious commitment of time and energy in moral reflection. Consultation with others whom we respect and trust can also prove to be an invaluable practice that encourages humility. Ultimately, the wisdom of our choices will largely depend on our level of maturity and on how well the character traits of honesty, sympathy, empathy, compassion, fairness, self-control, and duty have been integrated into our personality.

Integrity compels us to be socially conscious and other-directed, and to welcome both personal and professional responsibility. Its values encourage us to be honest in all our dealings and committed to a lifelong search for truth and justice. Its influence empowers us to be understanding rather than judgmental.

Integrity requires a self-discipline and willpower capable of resisting the seduction of temptation, whether in the form of desire, self-serving expediency, or deception. Integrity acts like a strong beacon in a storm to unerringly guide our actions throughout inner struggles and external conflict. Its priceless reward is peace of mind and true dignity. There's one proviso, however: no one can guarantee that his or her particular version of integrity is actually sound and true, and not misguided.

Just as the body needs oxygen to survive, the soul needs integrity. As we become more discerning, we learn to *feel* its rightness in our gut, to *know* deep inside that we're making the honourable choice.

Although competence and commitment play important roles, it is the manner in which we take a stand, the qualities of consideration, kindness, and heart-felt compassion, that others will appreciate and remember the most.

Developmentally, of course, we're not born with integrity. How well it is ingrained into our character depends on the healthy development of certain key personality traits, especially during the critical stages of early childhood. How well we maintain personal integrity once it develops depends thereafter on the strength of our values and the moral choices we make.

Integrity is built one small step at a time, yet it can slip away seemingly overnight. The popular expression "Don't sweat the small stuff" is bad advice in this context. If we are honest about small matters, we are more likely to handle the big issues in our lives with integrity.

The first time a teenager tries to smuggle a purchase past a customs officer, she may be doing it on a whim or a dare. If she manages to avoid getting caught, this option may start to look more attractive. "That was kind of exciting!" she might tell herself. It becomes easier thereafter to pad an expense account and rationalize that no one will notice: "Our taxes are so outrageous! We're one of the highest-taxed countries in the world!"

And so the best of intentions easily fade, to be replaced by worldly pragmatism and greed.

INTEGRITY IN ACTION

Integrity obliges us to become personally involved in actively doing something to right a wrong. If we are to do the right thing for the right reason, our motivation must stem from a desire to uphold our reasoned beliefs and societal values, not from any self-serving need to manipulate or impress others.

As persons of integrity, we *choose appropriate ways to express our anger.* If we perceive an injustice, we publicly state our position and proceed to protest or initiate some corrective action. This often means risking censure and rejection or even punishment if we choose to challenge an unjust law or practice.

We *choose to be reliable and predictable.* We are judicious in our choices, but once we have agreed to take on a task or job, we follow our commitments through to completion. Our desire is to serve, not to seek self-aggrandisement.

Unlike Stephen, we actively *choose to remain loyal* to our chosen partner. We commit ourselves to building a lasting relationship, one based on friendship, mutual nurturing, trust, and respect. We show appreciation and do not use or take our partner for granted. We seek to live a balanced and family-centred life.

We *choose to listen carefully to oppositional views* in order to show our respect, even though the opinions expressed may be radically different from our own. We reserve the right to remain sceptical and even suspicious of those we don't admire or have some instinctual or valid reason to distrust or fear. We continue to question and probe but do not gossip or twist others' words to serve our own purposes.

We *choose to be well informed* through examining and questioning the events, ideologies, and politics of our time. We think that it is important to formulate our own thoughts and opinions about global and moral issues. We keep current by reading and listening to the news and discussing important issues with others.

We *choose to learn from our own mistakes* and benefit from others' experiences, both good and bad. We are willing to apologize and then make amends to others whom we have wronged. The apology is not sincere if there is no change in our behaviour.

These are tough choices about whom and what to care about. In the ideal world, the path of integrity should reap rewards. In the grim realities of life, especially during turbulent times of conflict and war, keeping our integrity often comes at a terrible price. Sometimes the choice must be to remain patient, to wait out a dangerous situation, or even a regime.

SOME PERSONAL VIEWS OF INTEGRITY

A number of people I interviewed were invited to write down their thoughts about how they define integrity and to describe someone they admire who has integrity. They were also asked to explain the reasons for their choice. Several of those comments follow, and the thoughts of others appear throughout this book.

Alan, an accountant who specializes in fraud detection, describes integrity as "moral wholeness, a consistency of thought and action bound to a principle of honesty." He feels that absolute integrity is a god-like condition, and that none of us is without some integrity deficit. He writes:

> I know a man in whose company I feel privileged to spend time. He is, by most measures, an ordinary person, a successful businessman. I see nothing in him to suggest that this success was achieved by anything other than integrity, fairness, compassion and humility, and unstinting service to his customers. He is my counterpoint, my evidence to refute the view that business success can only be achieved through dishonesty and compromised principles.
>
> This man's conversation, like his behaviour, is direct and spontaneous, unguarded by contrivance, affectedness or pretentiousness. It is funny, it is warm, it is relevant, it is engaging; above all else, it is revealing. There is a transparency and consistency about what he says and does that reveals who he is, was and can be. Perhaps it reveals his soul. It allows communion and it invokes reverence and affection.
>
> He is what many people might see as an unsophisticated, poorly educated man. He mixes metaphors and pronounces big words with difficulty. He grew up in an environment where

integrity was not in abundant supply. He worked in a business sector characterized more by budget overruns, short deliveries, and shoddy workmanship than by integrity.

The man I admire loves life. He loves his family, his friends, the people he talks to in the checkout line at the grocery store, the person who pumps his gas. The man I admire loves truth.

Daphne, a high school teacher, writes:

I consider integrity as being honest with oneself and with others. To have integrity one must be strong, honest and loyal. Every effort must be made to do what one believes to be "right," and to have sound judgment in choosing the thought, word, deed or omission that is best in a situation. No matter the temptation, a person with integrity can be relied upon to stick to his or her principles, whilst maintaining an open mind and a flexibility of spirit.

My mum's integrity was something that I, as a child and adolescent, did not fully appreciate. Indeed for a long time I considered it the norm. It is only in later years that I have come to appreciate her strength and honesty. She regarded her word as her bond, and made frequent use of that expression. If ever she couldn't keep a promise, which was rare, she always provided a good explanation, and then made immediate preparations for an alternative arrangement.

She showed her integrity not only by what she did, but also by what she did not do. Mum refrained from gossip. She did not run people down behind their backs. She was not jealous of others. She was not excessive in anything.

Mum's life was not without adversity. In the last years of their marriage before my father's death, life was difficult due to his addiction to alcohol. She made every effort to support him through his various attempts to quit drinking. At the same time, she got on with her own life at a time when she could have been dragged down by depressing circumstances.

By being a loving wife to my father and a great mother to us, she maintained her independence by being an equal provider to the home. Mum took care of herself. She had help on a daily basis for housework, and she would rest every day for about an hour after work before she made supper for the seven of us. She delegated household tasks to us, teaching us responsibility not only by example, but also by providing us with involvement in the running of the house.

She was honest, industrious, generous, cheerful, loyal, efficient and frugal.

These two writers have been inspired in turn by the integrity of a co-worker and a parent, ordinary citizens living day-to-day lives. Too frequently, however, our view of integrity is shaken by the poor examples set by public figures who lose their personal and professional integrity. It's sometimes hard to keep faith when all around us people ignore or show disdain for the ethical and moral values that sustain a healthy society.

IS THE MEDIA CHANGING OUR VIEWS ON INTEGRITY?

Integrity reveals itself daily through generous acts of kindness, patience, good manners, law-abiding behaviour, and fair and honest transactions. Like spirituality, integrity needs a constant source of inspiration to nurture flagging intentions. This is especially true for children, but adults too can become disillusioned by rude or indifferent service providers, by tradespeople whose workmanship is careless and sloppy, by organizations with unfair business practices, by corrupt politicians – the list goes on.

Another serious source of disillusionment involves the media and its powerful influence on the way we view integrity in the broader world of public opinion. As Marshall McLuhan prophesied, the media has become the message. Whether we like it or not, our own view of integrity may be deeply affected by its disturbing news stories. Because the *loss* of integrity is big news, the grim details can quickly colour our worldview. Ironically, integrity itself gets only passing mention, usually in the obituaries or in some tribute honouring the passing of a well-known personality. It's a sad commentary indeed on the present state of morality that someone returning a wallet with everything intact is now a newsworthy item!

It's hard not to be cynical in this age of the anti-hero. "What's next?" we wonder as the radio clicks on for the morning news. We used to look forward to reading the newspaper over breakfast, but now we find ourselves reacting with outrage or great sadness to yet another dreadful report of people's inhumanity to others. Coverage of seemingly frequent episodes of the mass slaughters of innocent civilians tests the limits of our comprehension. Gruesomely graphic details of heinous crimes frequently turn our stomachs inside out. Murder is the ultimate rejection of integrity.

Where, and with whom, does the truth lie? The stories we read about powerful public figures often leave us with far more questions than answers. What's not being said in the article? Why did the reporter interview that particular individual but not his spouse?

We shake our heads and ask more probing questions. Why would people who seemingly had it all misuse their considerable power to commit fraud? Did these people at one time have integrity? Why did they not see beyond their false expressions of concern for the welfare of the company and its shareholders? Why did their peers trust them in the first place? Or why were those peers silent for so long?

It is tempting some days to avoid the media altogether. And yet remaining naive or ill-informed about the dark side of human nature is irresponsible. Evil must be acknowledged if we are to protect ourselves against its dangerous influence.

Certain stories persist in their impact, especially if children are involved – probably more than we realize. Sometimes these stories are just the tip of an iceberg. One such ongoing story, which first surfaced in 1997, involved youths and their coach playing the beloved Canadian game of hockey.

When Sam, a next-door neighbour, opened his morning *Globe and Mail* newspaper, the front-page headline jumped off the page: "Hockey coach pleads guilty to sexual assault charges."

Reading the article by reporter Alanna Mitchell, Sam experienced a mixture of horror and fear. Graham James, one of western Canada's most prominent junior hockey coaches, apparently confessed to 350 sexual encounters with two players, beginning in 1984 when the first player was fourteen and ending over six years later when the second player was nineteen. Allegations had come to light in the summer of 1996 when Sheldon Kennedy, a twenty-seven-year-old winger with the Boston Bruins, decided to go to the police. He had been receiving counselling for some time.

Sam's twelve-year-old son Kelly played in a local hockey league. Not surprisingly, Sam's adrenalin surged as he read highlights from the court records. Chief prosecutor Bruce Fraser reportedly "painted a picture of a man who bullied players into having sexual relations with him and callously abused his position of trust and his ability to further their careers." In one episode, James waved a shotgun. The assaults occurred in his one-bedroom apartment with some regularity on Tuesday and Thursday nights over a period of years while the boy was billeted with a family. Sometimes Kennedy would get off the telephone after James's summons and begin to cry, but the host family apparently encouraged him to go and "work it out" with the coach.

"What if Kelly has been exposed to any of this?" Sam wondered at the time. "How am I going to find anything out without alarming him and making him distrust all authority figures? When it comes right down to it, what do I *really* know about his coach?"

Several days later, Kelly's coach, a compassionate man named Brian, broke down in tears after reading another *Globe and Mail* article entitled "Kennedy: There are more victims."

David Shoalts quotes Kennedy. "It's just the shits trying to deal with what's messing up your head. You're just mentally screwed up, and it takes a while before you can get back to where you can trust and can feel."

Brian had no problem trusting his own integrity, but this scandal sickened him deeply. He found himself suddenly breaking out in a cold sweat. Did the parents of his players wonder about his intentions? Would they colour him with the same brush of suspicion and mistrust that had settled over the entire league?

The coach's concern raises an important issue. To what degree will a public that is regularly bombarded with such dark tales become grievously disillusioned and cynical enough to question whether there are any public figures left who have actually managed to keep their integrity intact?

THE DANGER OF PUBLIC DESENSITIZATION

With the recent widespread corruption scandals at corporate giants such as Enron and WorldCom, our trust rightly fades. When yet another CEO is charged, dismissed, or suspected of bringing down a company, we might hope that the magnitude of these crimes will cause us as a society to question whether our standards of conduct have slipped to a dangerous level and whether the business community is experiencing the legacy brought on by the cult of personality. Have our institutions become apathetic in the face of so much greed and materialism? More specifically, have we ourselves become desensitized to the point where we now minimize the significance of lost integrity in our own lives?

Corruption is often allowed to continue simply because no one wants to cast the first stone. Although the misuse of power to satisfy sexual obsessions is a common theme when integrity is lost, the Sheldon Kennedy story revealed another worrisome problem: the reluctance on the part of colleagues to judge a peer, even after it was acknowledged that James had severely damaged two innocent victims.

Will others guilty of similar wrongful acts take cold comfort in such public notoriety and continue to rationalize their own behaviour? Will their victims, the ones who have yet to confront their own perpetrators, be encouraged by similar stories to do so, or will they be left wondering whether there really is any justice in this world for the ordinary person? Justice is such cases seems questionable: one of the victims continued to suffer severe trauma some five years after the revelation, while the now-freed James was again coaching young hockey players in Madrid.

Will the victim worry, "What will happen to me if that abuser or fraud artist finds out that I went to the police or company authorities? Will he be able to find some way to seek revenge and punish me for doing the right thing?"

Guilt by association is yet another problem. People often reach faulty conclusions when they read a story because there is a tendency to personalize the news in order to understand and relate to it. Unprofessional behaviour in any field can, through the process of association, set the stage for broad suspicion. People may begin to question the integrity of their own doctor, dentist, lawyer, teacher, clergy, or politician. Employees may assess with a jaundiced eye a new recruit brought in to "save" the damaged company's reputation.

Public mistrust of the accuracy of the press only adds to this dilemma. No one in this day and age can afford to remain naive, to disown the healthy scepticism that makes us question what we read and see. To seek the truth, to sort out what is real from what is imagined or reported, is absolutely vital but increasingly difficult in this global and chaotic environment.

SELF-HONESTY: THE CORNERSTONE OF INTEGRITY

Self-knowledge is the essence of wisdom. Therefore, before going on to explore the key character traits necessary for integrity, let's do some reality testing.

How do you rate your own level of honesty? Your chances of being a person with integrity decrease with each "Yes" answer to the following quiz.

Overt Dishonesty

1 *You say and do the "nice" or evasive thing, instead of saying what you actually do feel, think, or want.*
What others think of you is overly important.

2 *You use stock phrases or glib, smooth-talking responses to get the answers or results that you desire.*
Accuracy or truth isn't your concern. You're a master at manipulating a situation to your own advantage.

3 *You automatically say what you think others want to hear.*
Pragmatism, doing what works, is your expertise.

4 *You say "yes" when you really don't mean it.*
In other words, you agree to requests from others with little or no intention of following through.

5 *You pick up subtle cues about what others want, and then second-guess their wishes.*
You don't bother to test out your presumptions by asking respectful questions about what the other person or persons would prefer before you proceed.

6 *You promise to do something by a certain date without regard to the time and logistics involved.*
You're not being honest with yourself. Being the "Pleaser" or "Mr Nice Guy" or "Ms Nice Gal" is all important, so you end up stressed out because you have to work extra hours to deliver on time.

7 *You no longer know what's true or real.*
You've lost track of who you are, or what you want. Along the way, you learned that it wasn't safe to tell the truth. Instead, it became easier to deceive and manipulate. Intimacy in relationships remains elusive.

While these manipulative forms of overt dishonesty may protect autonomy, independence, and privacy, such behaviours will also foster aloofness, secrecy, disrespect, and distrust in relationships. The welfare of others is rarely of concern here.

Covert Dishonesty

1 *You don't respond or participate in an on-going conversation.*
  You appear bored or distracted because you've gradually "tuned out." Preoccupied with your own thoughts, your mind has drifted elsewhere.
2 *You fail to verbalize your thoughts or feelings, and then get annoyed when others misunderstand or misinterpret you.*
  Others are magically expected to know your position, views, or intentions.
3 *You neglect to say what you would like to do or go to see.*
  Others are expected to be mind-readers, and then you complain if you don't like their choices.
4 *You "give in" and agree to do what others want just to keep the peace, and then you sabotage the event.*
  You go, but fail to participate. Or, at the last minute, you have a change of plans and cancel out.
5 *You agree to do something, then drag your feet about starting the job or project.*
  If it wasn't your idea in the first place, it's hard to get yourself motivated.
6 *You stubbornly procrastinate if you don't get your own way.*
  Stalling tactics, such as showing up alarmingly late, eliminate the possibility of an agreed-upon compromise.
7 *You set yourself up for confrontation or rejection by choosing something that is problematic for the other person.*
  You choose a present that suits your taste, or decide to go to some event or destination that you like, and then get moody when the other person doesn't seem to appreciate your gift, or doesn't appear to be enjoying the outing.

Neglecting to tell the truth and remaining silent are subtle but passive-aggressive forms of lying that leave the false impression that someone is being nice or easy to get along with.

In reality, this "pleaser" style of relating is not only vague and personally irresponsible, but the resultant misunderstandings typically breed lingering resentment and hostility. The pleaser's insensitivity and thoughtlessness further destroy trust.

2

Developing the Key Character Traits
of Integrity

A man does what he must – in spite of personal consequences, in spite of
obstacles and dangers and pressures – and that is the basis of all human
morality.

John F. Kennedy, *Profiles of Courage*

THE CONSCIENCE:
CARETAKER OF THE SOUL

Conscience is the sense of right or wrong within each individual.[1]

To be conscientious means honouring personal commitments and
obeying the rules that society has evolved for the public good.

A more formal definition views conscience as "the awareness of
the moral goodness or blameworthiness of one's own conduct,
intentions, or character together with a feeling of obligation to do
or be that which is recognized as good, often felt to be instrumental
in producing feelings of guilt or remorse for ill-doing."[1] Conversely,
wrongdoing is unlikely to produce feelings of guilt or remorse.

Like a sophisticated security system in our home, our conscience
monitors and evaluates our inner reactions and subsequent reactions, often after the fact. If we ignore its beeps and sirens, we do so
at our own peril.

---

1 This definition is based on *Webster's Third New International Dictionary*,
(1971) here vol. 2, 482.

A Healthy Conscience

As children, we don't have a clear sense of who we are and whether what we want is a good or bad thing. Through parental guidance, trial and error, and the hard knocks of experience, we gradually firm up the values we choose to live by.

Integrity plays a strong role in our adult personality only so long as we have come to believe and accept the value that a higher moral sense should ultimately prevail over any of our narrow-minded, self-serving motives. The epigraph to this chapter is a case in point. President Kennedy's message does not ring true, simply because we now know that in his personal life he chose not to "walk the talk," a too-frequent character flaw in our leaders.

The moral sense of what is considered acceptable behaviour grows out of what Adam Smith (1759) called the *natural* desire of people to be sociable, to be loved, and to desire the praise of others. Philosophers and poets down through the ages have supported the biblical dictum "It is not good that man should be alone" (Genesis 2:18). Affiliation is therefore a prime motivator in the development of a healthy conscience, because children are willing to do whatever is necessary to gain acceptance, praise, and approval from their significant others. As well, as sociologist Leon Festinger explains, children have a strong desire *to evaluate* themselves by comparing themselves to others – that is, unless there is some other objective way of doing so (Festinger, 117–40).

Thus children learn to anticipate what another person is thinking and feeling, and subsequently to second-guess what is expected of them so that those they admire will like them. When this need to affiliate isn't satisfied, their fears of disapproval and rejection escalate.

If this childlike dependency on external cues persists into adult life, as we will learn, second-guessing becomes a dangerous threat to the independent thinking so necessary for integrity – the choice to freely do the "right" thing, despite external influences.

Around the time of puberty, the approval of one's peers becomes of paramount concern. As self-control develops, teenagers learn to correct unacceptable responses so that others won't judge them harshly. In turn, they observe others' behaviour towards them and begin to question their own role in the interaction. Slowly, they form sound judgments about what is fair or acceptable behaviour. The Golden Rule "Do onto others as you would have them do onto you" gets played out in practice.

Through life experiences, people gradually refine their own values and judgments. They discover which values feel right and good and which judgments bring rewards or, conversely, lead to failure or rejection.

A Faulty Conscience

Much has been learned about a healthy conscience by studying the behaviour of people whose feeling capabilities have been severely damaged by some powerful trauma or ongoing abusive situation. The most extreme example of a faulty conscience is the amoral, psychopathic individual who fails to conform to the prevailing social and ethical standards of society. Guilt and fear do not register with these people, and the insight that is necessary for the psyche to take corrective measures is absent. Consequently, psychopaths show no real remorse or regret over their wrongdoing.

Psychopaths lack generosity because the positive emotions of sympathy, appreciation, and gratitude just aren't functioning. Ironically, these same emotions can be elicited from the other people psychopaths manipulate to feel sorry for them. Their bold promises, the ones that tell other people what they want to hear, are full of calculated lies and persuasive deceits.

Self-gratification is a driving force that motivates their every action. Poor impulse control means that they cannot delay gratification and their instinctual needs must be satisfied without delay. Many psychopaths are highly aggressive and often in conflict with the law. They tend to prey on vulnerable people who are weak, naive, or otherwise needy. Our prisons hold many who have committed heinous crimes. Some commit bigamy, but most drift in and out of relationships because they are not capable of true intimacy or genuine personal commitment.

The more passive and lethargic psychopaths sponge on society and on the people around them in a parasitic manner. In the world of a psychopath, integrity is a foreign concept.

MORAL DEVELOPMENT

The feelings that accompany the image of the mother's face, or her voice, or a bright toy rattle, are innately present at birth, while behaviours and standards of conduct are established over time.

Parents who wish to instil the values of integrity in their children are well advised to study the development of morality. An excellent source book is James Q. Wilson's *The Moral Sense*.

It is also important to understand that there are critical time periods when the development of certain traits can be enhanced or damaged.

Critical Periods

The Swiss psychologist Jean Piaget discovered that there are what he called "critical periods" in an individual's development when the psychological development of certain skills is maximized. Positive experiences during this specific period facilitate psychological development at an accelerated rate; negative influences retard growth or inflict serious harm. Before or after this particular period, the same positive and negative influences tend to be less traumatic.

Let's begin by looking at the critical periods for trust, guilt, and competence, the necessary building blocks of self-esteem upon which integrity is built.

Trust

The development of honesty is deeply affected by trust issues that are paramount in the second year of life. For example, if a child experiences painful memories of unmet emotional or physical needs during this time period, such as a prolonged separation or absence of a parent or caretaker, similar feelings of abandonment and grief can be reactivated and heightened at any stage of life.

Sometimes the hospitalization of the child may force a temporary separation. Thereafter, this child may experience acute anxiety and even panic attacks if similar feelings surface or are triggered by some loss. This distress can take the form of asthma attacks, episodes of claustrophobia, or ongoing hyperactivity. Trusting others

in adulthood may remain difficult unless the person becomes consciously aware of the dynamics of this early wound to the psyche.

Guilt

In the preschool critical period, children learn to internalize their
experience of guilt. Taking ownership of guilt is adaptive, because a
child can now recognize when his or her own behaviour has devi-
ated from the norm. A parent or sibling is no longer needed to
point out the transgression. However, if children are continually
denied some basic need or right, frequently ridiculed or shamed,
or dealt an unjust or cruel punishment inappropriate to a situation,
their development of recognition capabilities will be arrested.

If children are treated with dignity and respect, acceptable
behaviour is slowly ingrained with the help of parental instruction
or consultative questions such as: "Did you forget to say please just
now?" or "Do you think it's right to keep the money you just found
when it really belongs to your brother?" or "Did you wait for your
turn on the slide?"

Good guilt alerts the child to the insight that something isn't right.
Confidence and self-esteem build as more acceptable skills are
encouraged and positive feedback is given for good behaviour. Over
time, the likelihood of repeated offences gradually diminishes.

Any prolonged and wilful waywardness on the part of the child to
disobey a parent's reprimands and thus risk rejection can elicit
internal and generalized anxiety. When this child habitually fails to
make a correction or to apologize, guilt loses it corrective capacity
and becomes a prolonged negative state.

If children learn to expect censure from a critical parent, and to
fear punishment when they err, their anxiety becomes chronic.
Shame soon replaces guilt if a child is made to feel like a "bad person." This happens when the negative feedback dwells on character
faults rather than on the troublesome behaviour. The parent who
states, "Only a stupid ignoramus uses language like that" is attacking the child's character. A parent who says, "I don't like to hear
you swearing, Johnny. Perhaps you could count to ten to remind
yourself when you're tempted to use words like that," is trying to
correct the inappropriate language.

A complaint I hear frequently in my office goes something like
this: "That was Dad's favourite word: 'stupid.' I worked so hard at

school, but no matter how good my report card was, it was never good enough." One client, Robin, told me he eventually caved in to this pressure and quit school early. His present problems, not surprisingly, are related to issues around low self-esteem.

Competence

The critical period most relevant to integrity occurs between the ages of six and ten years of age when children are at school and their earlier expectations and responsibilities change.

During this period, reports Jerome Kagan in *Personality Development*, children in western society learn to develop "standards of rational thought and behaviour, autonomy, honesty, and responsibility" (155). Through intellectual mastery, he goes on, children learn attitudes that will affect whether they will anticipate success or dread failure.

At this critical stage, children are able to recognize standards of social competence. They establish relationships with teachers and learn to socialize with their primary reference group, their peers. They experience anxiety or guilt over such issues as aggression, their own and others' sexuality, and dependency.

Not only do children learn the major sources of anxiety during this period but they develop a preference for certain counteractive defences. After all, fear must be kept at a tolerable level. Unless they recognize that guilt signals a need to change behaviour, and are willing and able to acknowledge and accept expected standards, their ability to be honest will remain flawed.

THE KEY CHARACTER TRAITS OF INTEGRITY

Integrity requires us as adults to incorporate the values of honesty, sympathy, empathy, compassion, fairness, self-control, and duty into our character so that we will uphold high personal and professional standards in all circumstances.

Honesty

Honesty requires truthfulness, freedom from deception and fraud, and fair and straightforward conduct.

Words like *genuine* and *real*, *humble* and *loyal*, *reputable* and *respectable*, *creditable* and *praiseworthy*, *frank* and *sincere* are used to describe honesty. *Honour* and *integrity* are synonyms that indicate this uprightness of character.

To be truthful in essence means that we refuse to mislead others. While few would disagree that it is good to be honest and to follow society's well-established rules of conduct, many struggle with the concept that neglecting to tell the truth and remaining silent is a form of lying.

People often grow up in families where overt and covert dishonesty runs rampant. It's pretty hard to figure out what honesty is all about in such surroundings. Jean, an illustrator, was from such a family. Here's what he wrote about his first revelation that honesty mattered:

> It was thirty-six years ago. Maybe this small display of honesty means nothing. But to me, a kid whose primary role models were parents who lied in order to take advantage of every opportunity – even for fifty cents – it was an eye-opener.
>
> The first time I saw someone demonstrate integrity was two days after my best friend's fourteenth birthday. His father was driving us to an air show. At the entrance gate we saw a sign saying: *Age 14 and over pay adult prices*. We were both short and could easily have passed as thirteen or even twelve.
>
> It was our turn to pay. The ticket seller stuck his head in the car, looked at us, and asked my friend's dad, "They under fourteen?"
>
> "Nope. They're fourteen, and you should make them pay full price," the man said with a big smile.
>
> From observing this man over the years, I learned that he didn't have a sliding scale philosophy of "For a fifty cent gain you tell the truth, and for a five hundred dollar gain it's okay to lie." He acted the same way in all matters.

Searching for Truth

Honesty requires a never-ending updating of truth. To seek deeper and more profound truths is part of the maturation process. New experiences and circumstances often hurry this process along.

Mohandas Gandhi, known as Mahatma ("Great Soul"), described his search for truth in his book *Gandhi: An Autobiography*: "Truth is like a vast tree, which yields more and more fruit, the more you nurture it. The deeper the search in the mine of truth the richer the discovery of the gems buried there, in the shape of openings for an ever greater variety of service" (218).

Truth was never static for Gandhi. He tried to convince his followers of the principle of looking at things from different standpoints and from different circumstances. Compromise was therefore an important concept for him: "But all my life through, the very insistence on truth has taught me to appreciate the beauty of compromise" (148).

As a public figure Ghandi understood the danger of compromising the truth by asking others to believe a thing that he himself had not fully verified. By refusing to disguise his ignorance from his pupils, he presented himself as he really was: "A devotee of Truth ... must always hold himself open to correction, and whenever he discovers himself to be wrong he must confess it at all costs and atone for it" (350).

This seems a far cry from the public figures we read about in the newspapers who confess to a loss of integrity only *after* their wrong-doing has become public knowledge. An apology then is their last-ditch attempt to save face. Truly making amends for past mistakes, ones that have been damaging to others psychologically and often monetarily, usually requires a major change in character.

Integrity-seekers must be ever vigilant for bias in the media. In his autobiography, *Long Walk to Freedom*, Nelson Mandela likens this search for truth to an act of chasing elusive shadows. He eloquently describes the media as "only a poor shadow of reality; their information is important to a freedom fighter not because it reveals the truth, but because it discloses the biases and perceptions of both those who produce the paper and those who read it" (177).

Conflicting pressures, politics, and government-sponsored censorship make integrity difficult to maintain for those covering disasters such as the horrendous attack on the World Trade Center in New York. As viewers, we're left with the crazy-making task of discerning what is real from what should not be believed.

Troubling questions rarely have clear answers. Barry Allen, reviewing Michael Lynch's *True to Life: Why Truth Matters*, supports Lynch's view that beliefs, like any majority or authority, may be wrong, that objective truth transcends belief and consensus. Allen himself suggests that we discipline our credibility by a few simple rules: "Respect evidence; expect to hear reasons; be impartial, open-minded, sensitive to detail; and expect the same from others, whether personally or in the media."

The Naked Truth

In our personal lives, the way we say things can be just as important as what is said. Northrop Frye in *The Educated Imagination* distinguishes what he terms "the naked truth" from that which society has censored and deemed acceptable. Frye warns that even in truth there are certain things that can and cannot be said: "The words you use are like the clothes you wear. Situations, like bodies, are supposed to be decently covered" (57). This becomes a moral issue, according to Frye, when what is said is only partly true, or is misleading because it is slanted, false, or hypocritical in its intent. He suggests that the virtue of saying the right thing, at the right time, has become more important in our current social standards than telling the whole truth or neglecting to tell the truth at all. Even our libel laws "protect" us from the truth.

Honesty is considered laudable when we risk harm to ourselves but less so when others are put at risk for our own benefit, states lawyer Stephen Carter in his book, *Integrity*. Carter tells the story of a man, married for fifty years, who confesses on his deathbed that he had an affair thirty-five years before. "Arranging his own emotional affairs to ease his transition to death, he has shifted to his wife the burden of confusion and pain, perhaps for the rest of her life" (53).

In Carter's view, attempting honesty at a time when there is no risk of repercussions is simply a form of "fake" honesty, one that completely lacks moral integrity. It is obvious to him that this man's peace of mind and self-interest were of primary importance to him, not his love for his wife.

The Disguises of Truth

It is a tricky business to sort out what something actually means as opposed to what is being said. When our friends are in an emotionally charged state, we may question the validity of their exaggerations and superlatives. Or, we may wonder what it means when an acquaintance retreats emotionally into a moody sulk. This cloak of ambiguity reveals little concrete information.

As our senses are assaulted daily by advertising rhetoric, political pitches, and catchy slogans, we need to cultivate healthy scepticism to sort out fact from fiction. Abstractions and euphemisms in the form of jargon or cliché further complicate this task of discerning truth because there are no direct statements to clarify the real issues. What does *politically correct* actually mean? Fancy words like *downsizing* and *re-engineering* usually hide the grim reality that people are going to be fired. This jargon leaves the public unclear as to what's actually going on in that company.

"Plastic words" is what Uwe Porksen, a German linguist and Orwell scholar, calls words such as *developments, norms,* and *indicators.* Heather Menzies in *No Time: Stress and the Crisis of Modern Life* cites Porksen's view that because such words come from the worlds of technology, economics, or administration, they carry an authority, rigour, objectivity, and unassailability that in reality conveys no intrinsic meaning, yet implies that everything is under control: "Like brands and logos, they are a language of ready-made meaning that can be mobilized in an almost virtual form of public dialogue while masking the fact that very little has been communicated, explained or justified" (210).

Double-speak is alive and well, and sometimes even comical. In disbelief, we wonder: "Am I really hearing someone say that?" I listen as a speaker at a Canadian Centre for Ethics and Corporate Policy luncheon meeting says: "The answer is only true at the extremes." What exactly am I and the rest of the audience to make of this vague statement?

Or, in response to another enquiry, the same speaker says. "Let me reposition that question." This diversionary tactic reveals a lack of respect because it belittles the questioner's request for clarity.

The practice of inserting the words "always" or "never" into a sentence automatically lessens the likelihood that truth is being told. It also casts doubts in the mind of the listener as to whether the rest of the message is credible. "I would trust you with my life," Harry says to his friend after hearing one of his "always" sentences, "but I have no faith in your numbers!"

When is poetic licence appropriate? When storytellers embellish a tale to entertain or engage their listeners, they enhance the audi-

ence's ability to more vividly imagine the sights and sounds being
described. Their special tale-telling skills are acknowledged, so
there's no intent to deceive. But hyperbole used in another situation can turn darkly sour when such embellishments are used to
blame someone or something else, "to paint them black." When
such distortions manipulate the truth, it's not surprising that normally rational discussions get twisted into fierce arguments that
escalate into vindictive aggression.

SYMPATHY, EMPATHY, AND COMPASSION

Let's listen as this health-care worker links the attributes of sympathy, empathy, and compassion as she tells me about a colleague and
friend of twenty years:

> I believe my friend has strong and definite feelings about things
> and these feelings tend to control her actions. I truly believe
> that she could not defy her gut feelings without becoming physi-
> cally ill.
>
> A loyal and dedicated wife, she is very clear about the equal
> commitment both partners must have in a marriage. A mutual
> friend had recently gone through a separation, and in conversa-
> tion [Lillian] conveyed her pain and sorrow for both, for what
> they had lost from their lives, and the devastation the children
> must be feeling. She actually referred to it as a "death." Her focus
> was on the breakdown of this "sacred union" rather than the
> gossip that was circulating as to why this relationship had ended.
>
> As a mother, she *listens* to her children; she looks them
> straight in the eye and does not say a word until they actually
> stop talking. She constantly gives them a reassuring touch, a
> stroke on the head or a hug.
>
> One evening when we were over at their home visiting, Lillian
> came downstairs with a pained look on her face after tucking
> her children in bed. She had just told one of her kids that he
> couldn't do something he had requested. She conveyed her
> struggle to us. Her heart wanted to allow her son to do "what-
> ever," but her head told her he would be better off not doing it.
> She stuck with her feeling of what was best for his well-being.
>
> About a year ago, Lillian was working part time in an office
> where she did not agree ethically with how business was being

conducted. I sensed she was very upset about what she was being asked to do. Her "soul" wouldn't let her continue, no matter how much she tried to rationalize it. Her usual sense of contentment and well-being seemed to be in turmoil. In the end, Lillian quit her job, and found a new one. Her inner peace returned. I admire her for this.

As a friend, she is someone I can always count on. She loves being with her husband, and just as much, enjoys her time with the girls. She is happy being a "mom," and her profession is equally important.

Lillian demonstrated to her friend sympathy to the separated couple, empathy for her son's pain, and compassionate understanding of her own need to maintain high ethical standards.

SYMPATHY

Sympathy enables a person to be deeply affected and concerned about the well-being of others, to imagine their suffering, and be moved by their experiences.

Sympathy opens us up to the realization that others are suffering and experiencing grave pain or sorrow. This emotional connection can move us to tears when we witness the helpless victims of tragedies, disasters, and disease. Such sensitivity restrains us from acting cruelly or retaliating meanly when others offend or harm us. It moves us to serve others rather than use people and allows us to resist the temptation to act only in our best interests.

Feeling sorry for others, however, can be condescending, if we assume a superior position *above* the less fortunate. Sympathy becomes distorted when, as several clients have confessed, they feel a weird sense of elation or *schadenfreude* superiority when news reaches them about a colleague who has just been diagnosed with a grave illness.

Jeremy, a highly competitive workaholic, sheepishly admitted: "When I heard that Philip had cancer, part of me felt elated." Jeremy still had his health and stamina, while Philip's opportunities on the hierarchical ladder would likely be curtailed, or possibly even cancelled out by death.

It's hard not to disapprove of Jeremy's admission but important to understand that recognizing a competitive edge gives him a surge of power, an adrenalin high. (Adrenalin, by the way, plays a significant role in the addiction of workaholism.) Only through rediscovering his Feeling side will Jeremy be able to choose heart-felt empathy over this distorted form of sympathy.

EMPATHY

> Empathy is a "joining with" experience, an emotional yet objective accompanying.

Empathy is the capacity to "walk in another's moccasins," to get inside others' experiences, to share in their feelings of pain or joy. We find ourselves swelling with pride along with an Olympic athlete as she steps up to the podium. Our tears of joy match hers.

However, some people lack the emotional capacity to truly empa-thize and be able to conceive of the suffering that others go through. And there are some tragedies so utterly beyond belief that no life experience or imaginative skills can possibly prepare us to grasp their horror. We must first distance ourselves in order to gain enough objectivity to be able to absorb such atrocities, without becoming fascinated and succumbing to their awesome pull.

Carl Rogers founded a therapeutic client-centred model that emphasized genuineness, empathy, and unconditional regard. As a student, I remember reading his warning that in working on the back wards of a psychiatric hospital, he once flirted with his own breakdown. He tried to accompany his patients to wherever their feelings led them, no matter how powerfully deep, destructive, or abnormal they seemed. The question became – how could he be empathetic without crossing the fine line into his own madness?

Empathy requires a strict observation of ego boundaries. We can appreciate another's distress or elation without overreacting, because we remain a distinct and separate Self who can only imag-ine another individual's reality.

Empathy recognizes whose pain it really is. Feeling-type people often suffer needless pain because they lack Thinking's objectivity. They easily absorb someone else's trauma as if it were their own.

Taking everything personally is not a healthy or useful form of feeling. It is empathy that moves us to perform compassionate acts.

COMPASSION

Compassion is a form of spirituality, a way of living and walking through life.

Matthew Fox's views on compassion are expressed in his book *A Spirituality Named Compassion*: "It is the way we treat all there is in life – our selves, our bodies, our imaginations and dreams, our neighbours, our enemies, our air, our water, our earth, our animals, our death, our space and our time" (30).

Compassion must not be confused with altruism gone wrong, the love of another at the expense of oneself. Instead, as Fox clearly states, in compassion self-love and other-love are one.

Genuine compassion is generously given, with no strings attached. Altruism, on the other hand, can be motivated *solely* by self-interest. If someone gives to a charity and then actively seeks public praise for the gift, or helps a sick friend because she can be counted on to return the favour in the future, this is opportunism falsely masquerading as compassion.

Fortunately, people do tend to save their praise for those individuals who rise above self-interest, who help fellow citizens or strangers in need of assistance without fanfare.

Lapses of compassion became more understandable when we learn that people are more likely to help others who are similar to themselves and to intervene when they are alone rather than in a group. In the infamous Kitty Genovese case, reported by B. Latane and J. Rodin in the *Journal of Experimental and Social Psychology*, a young woman was stabbed to death in New York in 1964 while many apartment-dwellers watched. No one intervened or even called the police. The public outrage at this indifference fostered numerous experimental studies investigating *who* would help whom, and under what circumstances. Findings showed that where a number of other people were present or perceived as likely to become involved, individuals apparently felt a diminished responsibility to come to the aid of a "victim" in need.

As children, our innate sociability may foster the desire to be loved and admired, but true compassion for others must be learned. Through exercising this trait, we may inadvertently earn the respect and acceptance that we so ardently crave.

FAIRNESS

To be fair-minded requires honest and just dealings and decision-making that is reached through impartial and disinterested objectivity.

People can be fair without being sympathetic. Integrity, however, encompasses both traits.

Fair conduct requires that we be guided by the rules of governance and the moral standards of society. Our struggle is to stay free from personal bias and favouritism by being alert to the consequences of our decisions and choosing to do the right and equitable thing so that both parties stand to benefit.

There are many temptations that can threaten the generosity of fairness. We may choose to be fair simply out of self-interest or because of the fear of embarrassment, punishment, or reprisals if someone exposes our inequitable dealings. Or, we may decide whether or not to cheat based on what others are doing, or what is considered an acceptable norm or form of entitlement by our peers.

Fixed ideas and rigid stances are rarely fair, especially when they ignore individual differences. Rigidity can cause undue hardship for innocent others.

If children remain ego-centred and impaired by excessive self-interest, they will lack the sympathy and compassion necessary to know what is or is not fair. When a toddler such as Amantha expresses a preference for a toy she is hugging with the words "mine," she is not only claiming ownership of what she deems her personal property but she wants an exclusive title to it. Inevitably, a moral dilemma is forced upon her when her brother Timmy exerts similar rights over that same toy.

Later school experiences teach Amantha that two children cannot both win first prize in a spelling bee. Timmy too discovers the frustration of not being chosen to be the first in line to try out a new slide in the schoolyard.

It is a jagged learning curve for these youngsters gradually to discover not only what is fair in this world but also what they can reasonably expect to get away with. They learn early that variables such as age, size, and the authority that each party possesses must be factored into what is considered fair.

Hovering above such consternation is Amantha's dilemma of how she can look out for herself but still please her parents. After all, these folks hold the trump card – the stamp of approval or rejection.

Along the way, Timmy encounters various forms of fair play. He learns to take turns. As he matures, he can use chance to draw lots by flipping a coin. If a compromise doesn't work, sometimes a parent or teacher must step in to mediate the ensuing brawl.

While children seem to have an innate sense of fairness, the more sophisticated skills of cooperation, equity, reciprocity, and impartiality must be learned and applied as we mature.

COOPERATION

Cooperation is achievable when the importance of gaining the approval of others far outweighs the risks involved in losing a friendship or suffering a dreaded rejection. Around the age of four, children finally recognize the benefits of sharing. As their impulse control develops, they are able to delay gratification. They are willing to suffer short-term losses for the long-term gains of friendship and the possibility of future reciprocity.

Children learn to obey rules to please others, but the lure of instant gratification and unspoiled pleasure remains seductive, and they are tempted into testing limits. These mischievous actions not only get others' attention but also set certain people on edge – often a fun thing to do. Without strict discipline at an early age, children can become wilful and manipulative in the process of exploring other people's limits of tolerance.

"How far is too far?" becomes a practical life lesson. Children must discover the delicate balance between determining what behaviours meet their needs, measured against the possible losses that will be incurred if they push too hard.

EQUITY

Equity is the component of fairness that examines worth and merit. It is often represented by the proverbial weigh-scales of justice.

James Wilson explains: "In modern equity theory, a division of something between two people is fair if the ratio between the first person's worth (his effort, skill, or deeds) and that person's gains (his earnings, benefits, or rewards) is the same as the ratio between the second person's worth and gains" (60-1).

It is important to note that fairness doesn't always mean that people are treated as equals. Parents and children do not have equal power. Another common exception is progressive taxation in which the rich are expected to bear a heavier burden than the poor.

RECIPROCITY

Reciprocity requires give and take, a mutual exchange or interchange in kind or degree. It's a fair exchange if people reciprocate and repay by returning something that was said to them, done to them, or given to them. Integrity plays a strong role here, because reciprocation isn't appropriate when the message sent is an abusive statement rather than a compliment, a neglectful action rather than a thoughtful deed, or a token gesture instead of a sincere gift.

A further complication arises because no one can predict how others will respond. People are all different. For example, some are quite happy to give and expect nothing in return. Others become quite uncomfortable and even distressed at receiving something unless they can return the favour.

IMPARTIALITY

Impartiality permits no favouritism or bias to interfere or cloud an issue. We are more likely to comply with a decision, a sentence, or a verdict or to pay back what we owe in retribution if we believe that the proceedings leading up to a final decision were conducted in a fair manner.

The opportunity to present our own side is paramount. We want to be heard *and* understood. A traffic ticket found under our windshield wiper is annoying, but if we are persons of integrity we will accept that it isn't fair that our unpaid parking prevented others from using that meter. If there are extenuating circumstances, we still have the right to defend ourselves in court.

In contentious situations where negotiations and mediation are necessary to resolve issues between parties, impartiality helps to ensure that a practical and legitimate settlement can be reached independent of each side's will. Otherwise, personality is apt to dominate the negotiations, especially when one party takes a fixed take-it-or-leave-it stance and the other chooses to remain flexible, generous, and open to compromise.

In *Getting to Yes: Negotiating Agreement without Giving In*, Roger Fisher and William Ury of the Harvard Negotiation Project suggest some objective criteria that can be used to argue fairness: "market value, precedent, scientific judgment, professional standards, efficiency, costs, what a court would decide, moral standards, equal treatment, tradition, reciprocity" (89). The authors also offer some wise suggestions for establishing fair standards:

1 Frame each issue as a joint search for objective criteria.
2 Reason and be open to reason as to which standards are most appropriate and how they should be applied.
3 Never yield to pressure, only to principle. (91)

Fairness is rarely simple. Throughout history, citizens have started revolutions because the status quo was not fair. Unfortunately, life itself is not always fair. How many times do you and I shake our heads and ask, "Why do bad things happen to such good people?" "Why do natural disasters strike indiscriminately and leave one family intact, another destroyed?" "Why do illness and misfortune come to those who least seem to deserve it?"

Some people who find themselves in dire circumstances never manage to reconcile such injustice. Their psyches remain permanently scarred by disillusionment in the fairness of life, and they carry their anger and festering wounds forever unhealed.

Integrity cannot flourish when resentments linger and fairness turns into an ugly mentality of "tit for tat."

SELF-CONTROL

Self-control describes the capacity to resist improper or excessive desires, to judge what is best under the circumstances, and act accordingly, even when tempted to do otherwise.

Self-control saves us from a life of excesses, from blind ambition and greedy avarice and addictions to work, alcohol, nicotine, drugs, food, and sex.

Parents who are affectionate and consistently firm in their discipline create a safe environment wherein limits can be set and rules established for learning socially appropriate behaviours and an etiquette that shows consideration for others. For children to accept these instructions, they must be seen to be fair and not overly restrictive of self-expression. Parental praise, encouragement, and example curb and shape the child's natural instincts for wilful waywardness and rebellious protest. As self-control builds and the child learns to appreciate that long-term rewards are often worth waiting for, the ability to delay gratification becomes more attractive.

Willpower can't completely free us from negative social conditioning, but self-determination is an act of will that makes it possible for us to build in restraint and caution before we act, to think before we speak.

However, self-control is a moral virtue only so far as our intentions are praiseworthy. James Wilson rightly points out that while petty thieves are impulsively aggressive and desirous of a quick and easy reward, professional criminals who are found guilty of embezzlement often display a great deal of self-control as well as an ability to delay gratification, often for long periods of time: "while we may admire the skill with which they operate, we do not regard this skill as a sign of virtue" (Fisher and Ury, 80–1).

DUTY

Duty is the value that motivates people to freely honour their personal obligations and to steadfastly abide by societal laws.

Moral laws spell out the socially acceptable behaviours considered necessary to establish law and order. We have a duty as citizens not only to honour these obligations but also to serve others so that good and wise ends can be achieved.

Children perform assigned duties to please their parents and receive praise. As adults, many people carry out their mandatory responsibilities simply to avoid being caught. They're afraid of the consequences of failing to pay their taxes or disobeying the rules of the road. Moral duty, on the other hand, rises above such self-interested gratification or solace. An ingrained sense of duty compels us to act without being intimidated by fear or tempted by the promise of a reward or acknowledgment, no matter what the degree of difficulty or inconvenience.

Duty can be deadly without a spirit of generosity and a sense of fun. We hear its solemn pronouncements and authoritative voice whenever we bark out commands that contain the controlling words "you should" or "you should not." Misused, duty can be a super-ego watchdog on a power trip!

Duty, on the other hand, can guide our spirit of good will. Under its influence, we willingly choose to keep our word and follow through on our promises, honour our commitments, and keep our fidelity.

We tend to honour and respect those who are of consistent and predictable character, who possess an ingrained sense of duty and conscience that motivates them to volunteer their time and energy to do charitable good works that improve the quality of others' lives, or choose to serve their country in troubled times. We also admire those who refuse to betray others or divulge secrets. Conversely, we hate to see people – the slackers, cheaters, liars, and thieves – who ignore their sense of duty and yet still manage to "get away with murder!"

RE-EVALUATING OUR VALUES

"Where did that idea come from?" I ask my clients. "Who taught *you* to value that? What do you personally believe today?"

Instead of blindly following what we've been taught in childhood, we need to re-examine our values with fresh objectivity and "big picture" vision, not from a child's myopic self-focused bias. Truly mature adults take personal ownership and responsibility for choosing what they believe in, what they discover is morally true and acceptable.

L. Joseph Stone and Joseph Church in *Childhood and Adolescence* describe the child's maturational growth: "His emotions become more stable, and, while remaining strong, are tempered, controlled, and integrated ... he gains in mature flexibility." Not bound by habitual ways of thinking, the child can take a fresh look, consider new evidence, and tolerate challenges to his assumptions. It takes willpower to change with the times, to shed questionable or obsolete values and principles, and to remain enthusiastic while developing new tastes, interests, new friends, and even careers. The authors conclude: "He can make such changes and still hold fast to such fundamental values as esteem for human feelings and integrity" (516–17).

The choices we make will determine whether our version of honesty and truth prevails over deception and manipulation, whether sympathy and empathy colour our decisions, and whether fairness wins out over self-interested greed.

Self-control and duty, with a strong dose of humour and humility, go a long way to ensuring that our integrity strengthens and grows as we mature.

3

A Philosophical Look
at Integrity

The life which is unexamined is not worth living.
Socrates

THINKING ABOUT THINKING

For a deeper understanding of the underpinnings of integrity, it is helpful to explore some philosophical views on morality, ethics, and values. A short but somewhat ponderous description of this complex field in *The Oxford Companion to Philosophy* states that philosophy is "rationally critical thinking, of a more or less systematic kind about the general nature of the world (metaphysics or theory of existence), the justification of belief (epistemology or theory of knowledge), and the conduct of life (ethics or theory of value)" (Honderich, 666).

As a novice who has always been intrigued with philosophical questions, I began to read with an honest curiosity but soon found myself – a psychologist, from a relatively recent discipline, wandering around in another related but ancient one – daunted by the depth and richness of this fascinating field of study.

I hope these brief highlights will be of some assistance to other neophytes wishing to be similarly enlightened.

DIFFERENTIATING TERMS

A brief glossary of terms relevant to the study of integrity follows.

Morality

Morality concerns the establishment of a set of moral principles or rules of conduct.[1]

Morality relates to the principles of right and wrong behaviour that society deems acceptable, but these rules of conduct are understood rather than being written out for all to see. Cultural norms are established through scholarly and legislative study that identifies what behaviours are considered virtuous and worthy of wide acceptance, and what vices are to be shunned rather than condoned. Here the diversity of multiculturalism presents cultural and ethnic differences that must be taken into consideration.

Our personal moral sense is shaped by the instructions we receive in early childhood at home and at school and through exposure to religious teachings. Thus morality guides our reactions to the world around us, and we gradually formulate judgments about how others should or should not act. While the moral choices we make help define our character, the swirling influences of external circumstances too frequently warp our best intentions.

Our possession of a moral sense is inescapable and fundamental, says Iris Murdoch in *Metaphysics as a Guide to Morals*. It is the demand that we be virtuous, that we seek "something higher." Unfortunately, there are people such as psychopaths who are not guided by these strong moral principles, and others who struggle out of ignorance or naivety.

Values

Values underlie the intent or motivation of a person's actions.

The term "cultural norm" is an expression of what society as a whole ought to treasure or, conversely, devalue.

Values, according to *Webster's*, concern the personal evaluation of the relative worth, utility, quality, status, excellence, or importance attached to a person or thing. Each person determines what he or

1 Definition based on Webster's *Third New International Dictionary* (1971).

she considers admirable, worthwhile, or desirable; but obviously the privilege of choice carries with it a grave responsibility when it comes to acting with integrity. What is actually correct, what is the truth?

The clash of values and diversity inherent in a multicultural society adds complexity to our choices. Tolerance, the authentic acceptance of differences that deviate from a standard, makes it more difficult for us to evaluate what constitutes a virtue or vice. We must learn to tolerate conflicting ideas on practical or even humanitarian grounds without embracing all ideas as equally acceptable. Evaluating the wisdom of our choices is an integral part of integrity. Through example and instruction, we learn to allow our standards and values to guide our behaviours and actions. Rebels who upset the norm by expounding a different set of accepted beliefs present a fresh challenge to our own beliefs and attitudes.

Philosophical concerns typically focus on determining what particular property or characteristic gives something its value. Other inquiries question whether value is to be found in the object itself or in how people feel towards it. Of interest to philosopher Isaiah Berlin was whether a system of values can or should be internally consistent. Michael Ignatieff, in *A Life of Isaiah Berlin*, summarizes Berlin's thoughts on this subject: "The conflict of values – liberty versus equality; justice versus mercy; tolerance versus order; liberty versus social justice; resistance versus prudence – [is] intrinsic to human life" (285).

Berlin indicates that liberty must be given priority to ensure choice, but that under certain circumstances, liberty might need to be curtailed in the interest of social justice.

Ethics

Ethical principles relate to the execution of moral duty and obligation.[2]

2 These definitions are adapted from Webster's *Third New International Dictionary* (1971) and the course book *Codes of Ethics, Conduct and Practice* by Max Clarkson, Michael Deck, and Richard Leblanc, Faculty of Management, University of Toronto, 1996.

This branch of philosophy uses ethical reasoning to make decisions about what *should* be considered right and good, or wrong and bad.

A *code of ethics* is a *statement* that sets out the guiding principles and values for professional standards of conduct. The business, academic, and artistic worlds establish these ethical standards in order to guide people's actions and to settle disputes.

A *code of conduct* is a *list of rules* that spells out what one should or should not do, and it is usually included in the ethical statement.

A *code of practice* is an *interpretive guide* that outlines how values and principles should be carried out in a particular setting, such as a corporation or institution.

Although habits form easily, the character trait of integrity requires a lifetime of directed effort, healthy scepticism, and true vigilance in times of adversity and temptation. Ethical and moral dilemmas often challenge our old uninformed beliefs and superstitions. Consequently, a curious mind is an invaluable asset, stimulating us to think in new ways. Although we lack the analytical and argumentative skills of a Socrates, or his keen ability to scrutinize and refute false beliefs, we can at least consciously strive to remain open and flexible when examining the status quo.

As Seth Godin points out in his book *Wisdom, Inc.*, the two-thousand-year-old Hippocratic Oath has remained viable across time simply because it offers "a flexible framework for medical ethics instead of a rigid set of rules" (41). Of course, some pro-life advocates would obviously not agree.

PHILOSOPHICAL THOUGHTS, PAST AND PRESENT

Philosophers through the ages have debated the question of exactly how people make moral decisions and determine truth. They have generally agreed that there are three necessary elements to this search: knowledge, understanding, and a guiding wisdom. Philosophers differ, however, around the question of how truth itself is determined.

The Athenian philosopher Socrates (470–399 B.C.) believed that knowledge is the "moral virtue of man" alone, but that a divine voice within us guides our actions. Today we would call that voice our conscience.

Although Socrates did not record his thoughts, his devoted pupil Plato wrote passionately about his teacher's life and dogma. Above his own life, Socrates valued his conscience and the search for knowledge. Ultimately he was executed because he dared to challenge others' absolute truths.

Plato's early dialogues record Socrates's question-and-answer method of philosophizing. Socrates acted as a critic, "eliciting opinions from his interlocutors and subjecting them to critical scrutiny, usually resulting in a refutation by showing the doctrine in question to be inconsistent with other propositions agreed upon by both parties to be true." He often feigned ignorance as a way of subverting over-confident, self-professed experts (Honderich, 837).

In his introduction to *The Republic of Plato*, translator Francis Mac-Donald Cornford states that Plato compared the practice of morality to the art and craft of medicine, navigation, or shoemaking. He adopted Socrates's belief that there should be an *art of living* that would be analogous to a craftsman using his knowledge to build a house and thereby achieve a purposed end. Plato goes on to clarify: "Similarly a man can live well only if he knows clearly what is the end of life, what things are of real value, and how they are to be attained ... If a man imagines that the end of life is to gain wealth or power, which are valueless in themselves, all his actions will be misdirected."

Plato also believed that society must be ruled by leaders who have "learnt, by long and severe training, not only the true end of human life, but the meaning of goodness in all its forms" (8–9).

WHAT IS THE SOURCE OF TRUTH?

Our search for truth over the centuries has led to widely divergent philosophical views. Philosophers founded their own schools of thought, each devoted to its own theories, concepts, subjects of interest, practical issues, and debates. Early rationalists such as Aristotle (384–322 B.C.) studied the *origins* of ideas and beliefs and saw

rationality as the key feature distinguishing man from other animals. In formulating moral truth, rationalists emphasized the role
of *reason* along with intuition.

Aristotle's thoughts have influenced the terminology of philosophy itself. Concepts such as premise, conclusion, essence, metaphysics, potentiality, categories, and analysis, many of them
relevant to integrity, have been taken from Aristotelian writings
(Honderich, 50). Yet the Aristotelian emphasis on reason has
proven problematic. We will see later what happens when the
Thinking function dominates Feeling, as is the case in obsession,
and what that dynamic does to integrity.

Extreme empiricists. basing their knowledge on sensory experience that also included feeling, introspection, and authority, took a
more holistic approach. Two empirical philosophers whose work
contributed to the demolition of pure rationalism were David
Hume and Immanuel Kant.

David Hume (1711–1776), the Scottish philosopher, essayist,
and historian, suggested that because human nature places limits
on the capacity for scepticism, people cannot determine the relations of cause and effect or prove what is right and wrong by reason
alone. In *An Enquiry Concerning Human Understanding*, Hume wrote
that "all our ideas are nothing but copies of our impressions ... that
it is impossible for us to *think* of anything, which we have not ante-
cedently *felt*, either by our external or internal senses" (62).

Hume called consciousness the "influence of the will" and
declared that people learn from *experience* alone how one event constantly follows another. If our actions cause negative feedback and
effects, we learn to avoid similar circumstances, or at least understand that they are bad. Similarly, through observing others'
actions, customs, and gestures, we attempt to interpret motives and
inclinations. Using the process of inference and association, we
form an impression.

Hume cautioned that the human character is inconsistent and
irregular rather than constant. By making allowances for the diversity of character and the prejudices and opinions of different people, we can "form a greater variety of maxims, which still suppose a
degree of uniformity and regularity" (85).

Immanuel Kant (1724–1804) also struggled with causation, that
is, an act leading to an effect. He believed that sensory perception
and reason both inform the laws of morals – the conscience. Indi-

viduals act in accordance with moral law when they act in a kind and helpful manner simply because they know it will pay off. However, Kant felt that such actions were moral actions *only* if the person acted out of duty, not from any self-interested motivation.

Kant asks in *Dreams of a Spirit-Seer:* "Can one properly be called upright and virtuous who would gladly yield to his favourite vices if only he were not terrified of a future punishment, and would one not rather say that he avoids the expression of evil but nourishes a vicious disposition in his soul, that he loves the advantage of the simulation of virtuous action but hates virtue itself?" (Guyer, 9).

Kant called the ability to use practical reason to generate principles of conduct "the autonomy of the will." He believed that will constitutes the dignity of the person and that it must not be guided by self-deception.

However, it must be noted that what conscience dictates can vary from person to person, from culture to culture. Also, having a conscience is not the same as using it. It must be fully activated and possess a clear purpose.

Paul Guyer observes in *The Cambridge Companion to Kant* that no one played a greater role than Kant in "the transformation of the Western conception of a human being from a mere spectator of the natural world and a mere subject in the moral world to an active agent in the creation of both" (3). In other words, Kant believed in being proactive in making good things happen, a concept that plays a key role in a process I call Internalizing. This healthy way of problem solving and improving one's level of integrity is presented in chapter 10.

THE AGE OF ENLIGHTENMENT
AND INDIVIDUALISM

During the eighteenth century, along with the philosophy of Hume and Kant, the ideas of thinkers such as Newton, Locke, Adam Smith, and Voltaire influenced the intellectual movement called the Enlightenment. Its philosophy shifted the focus of morality and ethics from the group to the individual, thereby influencing every sphere of life and thought in virtually every European country.

Enlightenment doctrines championed the individual's use of his or her own reason to think, to speak freely, and to act correctly. Starting from the position that all people are created equal in the eyes of God, Enlightenment thinkers maintained that everyone had the right to claim equitable and fair treatment in law.

Personal freedom meant that integrity would not be dictated by a blind obedience to external authority but be guided by each person's rational thinking. Free inquiry challenged old sacred writings, traditions, and customs.

The movement encouraged sympathy, personal responsibility, and free inquiry. Personal liberty meant that people's compassion and sense of fairness were not reserved only for one's kind. This meant that cruelty to those different from oneself was no longer acceptable public behaviour. Slavery was finally acknowledged to be wrong.

In its search for new truths, however, the Enlightenment movement left a legacy that continues to undermine integrity.

NARCISSISM: INDIVIDUALISM GONE WRONG

The prevalence of narcissism in today's society is strongly influenced by the dark side of the Enlightenment. Individual freedom deteriorates into narcissism when there is insufficient self-control or compassion and no strong sense of duty to guide its actions. Once established, narcissism can become a destructive dynamic that warps life's energy and blocks psychological growth.

Narcissism, like extreme individualism, has utter disdain for society's collective values, rules, and regulations. Narcissists see themselves as special, set apart and above ordinary people.

They are indeed interesting people. Liam Lacey begins a review of a film adaptation of Leonard Cohen's *The Favourite Game* with this clever summation: "Narcissists, bless them, make it easy for the rest of us. They are never short of a conversational topic, save you the trouble of complimenting them, and do not need to be entertained." I have found that narcissists rarely ask questions of the listener in their one-way conversations. If they do, they rarely listen to the answers and quickly self-reference back to something *they* are interested in.

Intelligent and seductively charming when they want something, narcissists can be blindly ambitious and power hungry. Their manipulations can be cruelly destructive and cause others great suffering.

Why are narcissists at special risk of losing their integrity? The most important reason relates to the chief sign of neurotic narcis-

Institutions too can be narcissistic. Today, our disillusionment and cynicism grow as we witness our governments' myopic policies and self-serving leadership.

To do battle with this narcissistic focus on "me, my, and mine," society must once again promote core values such as love, integrity, personal and public responsibility, and equal respect for *all* human beings.

IDEOLOGY AND SELF-CONTEMPT

Another modern-day thinker, John Ralston Saul, suggests that self-loathing is the key to our present-day weakness for ideology. The aim of the ideologues is to bamboozle the majority into acceptance.

In *The Unconscious Civilization*, Saul calls the small, elite minority claiming to have the "truth" the *elect*. Their primarily loyalty is to their own group, and they think of the ordinary citizen with contempt, and discourage and even punish outspoken individualistic or democratic expression. The passive citizen who willingly sacrifices freedom of thought and unquestioningly accepts the elitist version of reality is in danger of slipping into an unconscious form of self-contempt.

According to Saul, the current obsession with modern management and corporatism was born in the nineteenth century as an alternative to democracy. These elite systems promoted the legitimacy of groups over that of the individual and were fostered by dictators such as Italy's Mussolini and Portugal's Salazar.

Illusion is prevalent in today's corporate society where technocrats are gods. Since the oil crisis in 1973, Saul explains, there has been no real growth; instead, only debt, inflation, and high unemployment. Yet the elite have built an artificial sense of well-being in which "truth is not in the world, but instead, it is in the measurements made by professionals" (9). Saul further warns that the French aristocracy, the Roman Empire, and the Russian elite were all in a similar state of effervescence before their fall.

Elitism also leads to demonization, the denial that there is any goodness or moral value attached to the other side. The violent skinheads in Germany who act out their own self-hatred by denigrating others are prime examples. Saul concludes: "To live within ideology, with utopian expectations, is to live in no place, to live in

sism: a damaged Feeling function. When the feeling side of the personality barely functions, the traits of sympathy, empathy, and compassion fail to inform the decision-making process. Instead, the Thinking function dominates, and its performance-oriented values are focused on building a favourable public persona that will broadcast success.

Narcissists therefore identify themselves with an idealized, inflated, and often arrogant view of what they wish to be – or more importantly, what they wish to be *seen* to be. This self-aggrandizing persona is who they believe themselves to be. Any information that conflicts with this perception of reality is quickly rejected or dismissed as irrelevant. Yet rarely do their actual accomplishments measure up; they glibly say and do the right thing to impress others, but their actions are manipulative and self-serving. Convinced that they are "right" and their way is "best," they hold stubbornly to their unique view of reality. Rarely do they show any interest in challenging those views by seeking others' opinions or beliefs.

In sharp contrast, integrity is about openness, not fixated ideas and ideologies.

Secondly, narcissists gradually opt out of personal responsibility. Like Tom Sawyer, they set up others to paint their fences. Their energy goes into highly visible, results-oriented actions. At any cost, they relentlessly pursue the power and wealth necessary to achieve their own self-serving ends. Spouses or assistants at work are *expected* to perform the mundane, ordinary tasks.

All situations must be finely controlled, because narcissists' ambitious goals are sacrosanct. Their self-focused false integrity is rarely concerned with the welfare of those outside their immediate circle, unless it is someone who is seen to be useful in some way. Anyone who threatens their illusionary superiority can expect to receive retaliatory rebukes or one-upmanship retorts or worse. This is especially problematic in a loving relationship. According to Sandy Hotchkiss in *Why Is It Always about You? Saving Yourself from the Narcissists in Your Life*, narcissists' relationships are all about exploitation. It is envy that causes them to be threatened by the very qualities that initially attracted them to their spouse but now make them feel inferior. A competitive spirit fuels their need to tear that person down and regain their superior position: "Envy leads to contempt and contempt to destruction, leaving Narcissists frustrated and empty in their pursuit of perfection" (111).

Thirdly, narcissists are the ultimate pragmatists. They embrace values and beliefs when useful and disregard them when they are seen to be counterproductive. Dissociation, a well-exercised defence mechanism, allows them to ignore people and things at will. Narcissists have problems trusting anyone, so a strong paranoid streak often complicates their vague morality and fluctuating value system.

Envy, the dark side of a competitive spirit, is a compelling motivator in determining their pragmatics. Surpassing the Joneses, not keeping up with them, is their goal. Anyone who threatens their illusionary supremacy can expect to receive retaliatory rebukes or one-upmanship retorts or worse. The career of a protesting colleague may be blocked. Sometimes devious game-playing tactics of revenge go on for years. When feelings don't work, forgiveness is a foreign concept. When those being manipulated finally get wise and start to confront the narcissist's selfish schemes and wavering promises, their just complaints are interpreted as "vicious" personal attacks. Narcissists then believe that *they* are being victimized. In fact, even having a different point of view or speaking one's own truth can elicit retaliatory reactions. In the paranoid narcissist world, two people can't both be right, so any disagreement means "You think I'm wrong!" The focus of attention must always stay on them.

Lastly, shame-avoidance plays a major role in their loss of integrity when too many things start to go badly and their unconscious insecurity roars to the surface. Their external frame of reference gives them an exaggerated fear of rejection, making them highly dependent on public approval and the affirmation of others. Because the authentic Self has disappeared into the persona, the self-awareness necessary for insight is sadly lacking. The crumbling defence systems that fed their cocky arrogance can no longer protect them from its polar opposite – unconscious self-doubt and self-loathing. They have little insight into what went wrong, and worse still, no real remorse, because the conscience cannot experience guilt without input from the Feeling function.

The powerful control that allows these emotionally crippled folks wilfully to do whatever they want is slowly undermined as once-powerful defences break down and the psyche forces a correction. Severe depressive symptoms and anxiety attacks begin to destabilize their effectiveness. Their acute fears generate extreme agitation,

which produces uncontrolled fits of rage and insidious m
swings. Secrecy and privacy become essential. It is the determ
tion to "save face" that now concerns the narcissist, not integrit

CULTURAL NARCISSISM

The exaggerated self-aggrandisement of narcissism can be obser
not only in the individual but also in western society itself.
The Culture of Narcissism, social critic Christopher Lasch sees spec
changes in our society and culture that parallel the pathology of
narcissistic personality.

Human beings have always been selfish, and groups have a t
dency to be ethnocentric, but Lasch believes that character dis
ders like narcissism are fast becoming the most prominent form
psychiatric pathology. Their emergence, he says, "derives fr
quite specific changes in our society and culture – from bure
cracy, the proliferation of images, therapeutic ideologies, the rat
nalization of the inner life, the cult of consumption, and in the l
analysis from changes in family life and from changing patterns
socialization" (74).

Lasch maintains that, like the narcissist, our contemporary c
ture depends on the vicarious warmth provided by others, yet
fears dependency. Its fascination with youth reveals an intense fe
of old age and death, along with a fatalistic attitude. Immedia
gratification has become a seductive force, and short-term thinkir
prevails.

Our society's ever-vigilant preoccupation with security make
position, power, and wealth the means to an end. The bottom lin
is sacred. Attaining one's goal is paramount, and exceeding it is th
next order of business. Purposeless play in general is not valued
At home, an ever-present competitive spark fuels power struggle
that sour male-female relationships. Being right is ultimately mor
important than being happy.

As a result of the spiritual vacuum of cultural narcissism, mean
ing is missing from our society. An inner emptiness prevails. Noth
ing is ever good enough – more is always better. As a consequence
we watch as frustrations grow unchecked and emotional turmoi
creates physical and psychological cravings that are left unsatisfied.
In the midst of societal chaos and despair, personal angst gets
played out in depression and anxiety.

limbo ... to live in a void where the illusion of reality is usually created by highly sophisticated rational constructs" (28).

The way to escape elite ideology, Saul suggests, is through real oppositions that involve our struggling between choices – between humanism and ideology, balance and imbalance, equilibrium and disequilibrium.

BEWARE OF TRICKERY AND DECEIT

In our own pursuit of truth, we must beware of ideologies that come wrapped in the seductive guise of simplicity. Often what isn't spelled out is the complexity of the key issues and step-by-step practicalities and strategies required to achieve a viable solution.

Free speech can echo in a vacuum of empty rhetoric. Charismatic ideologues try to catch our attention through the use of sound bites, symbols, and slogans like "the Common Sense Revolution." Expediency is another tactic. Democratic dialogue is impossible when demagogues rush their policies through, even while pseudo-hearings are held across the country. Professing to listen to their opposition, they proceed to do only what they want. In other words, they are doing the right thing – but for the wrong reason.

Desperate to find quick solutions for long-term problems, we are frequently overwhelmed by information overload. It is easy to be fooled by facts presented in absolute terms where things are either right or wrong; where subtleties and complexities are replaced by concrete "facts and figures." In a *Globe and Mail* article Harvey Schachter quotes journalism professor Michael Cobden: "One of the reasons people hate politics and the media is that they don't understand. They are made to feel foolish in their own eyes and that's not a nice feeling." Cobden says that the media assume most people have more understanding and background than they actually possess. When something has been explained for the first time, the media assume that everybody understands and will remember. But people don't remember, and they rely on the media to help them grasp the essence of problems, not confuse them with complexities falsely presented as simplistic. People do not want to be talked down to or patronized.

Choice does offer the freedom to oppose ideology, as John Ralston Saul suggests. Instead of being swayed by the promises of today's demagogues and extremists, society needs to support a healthy individualism, with its principles of a workable democracy where people are listened to and free electoral votes bestow the power necessary to remove leaders who do not have the best interests of the public, or the country, at heart.

On our part, we must be ever vigilant for signs of arrogance and greed in our leaders – a sure sign of individualism gone wrong.

In Part 2 our focus moves from an understanding of the essence and development of integrity within the individual and in society to an exploration of its tragic loss.

PART TWO

Why Do People Lose Their Integrity?

4

The Enemies of Integrity

We have met the enemy and he is us.

Walt Kelly, Earth Day poster, 1971

A cynical and rebellious disdain for integrity comes across loud and clear in the words of some self-professed doubters. These people have been disillusioned by some toxic experiences that continue to colour their views on the possibility of wholeness.

Chad, an ambitious stockbroker, responds, "I remember you once saying that you thought the loss of integrity was one of life's great tragedies, that by choosing to ignore society's moral and ethical standards we risk losing everything of real value. Well, I just don't have that choice. In this crazy world, you can't afford to do anything but look out for Number One. All the successful people I know lie and cheat and steal. Why should I turn myself into a patsy? The world today is dog eat dog. I'd rather eat than be eaten!"

Cherylyn, a bright human resources executive, offers her immediate thoughts after hearing Stephen's heartbreaking poem from this book's first chapter. "Stephen's problem is not the loss of integrity but the loss of perspective. He went too far. I know where to draw the line!" Later, on reflection, she admitted that the fine line is not always that easy to establish.

A radical university student thinks integrity is for someone else. François put it this way: "Modern morality is situational. There are no absolute rules of right or wrong any more. So why shouldn't I just make up my own? Besides, look around you. Personally I've never met anyone who is good enough to stand up on his soapbox and tell me what to do or not do. And what's more, I'm not about to give anyone else that kind of power!"

Frank, the president of an industrial design group, expresses his ambivalence on the subject:

> I rail at the thought of identifying people with integrity, because in my mind they don't really exist. I define integrity as an abstract dynamic that is displayed through living your values and being true to yourself and others. It's rarely measurable and not quantifiable. It can't be bought and it's transitory.
>
> Many talk integrity, but few deliver. Seemingly it's always under siege. We're seldom taught its importance, what constitutes it, or how to hold onto it. As a result, everyone has or sometime will compromise their integrity. Scratch the surface, and it will smell.
>
> People survive their flawed existence by living in their image rather than according to their values. They perform, weaving the web of deception, living how they want to be perceived rather than what they truly are.
>
> I believe people in their stupidity or naivety have moments or periods of integrity, where right is chosen over wrong. But, like a handful of sand, the harder you squeeze it, the more likely it is to slip away. What remains is well-intentioned people poorly suited to be role models in life.

These three people experience integrity as being "out there," an abstract dynamic, not an integral part of their self-perception. What has happened in their lives to make them so cynical, so clearly unable to trust the concept of integrity? We'll begin by exploring one of the major culprits that undermine this priceless trait.

ALIENATION AND THE LOSS OF INTEGRITY

Alienation is affiliation gone wrong.

If our innate need to belong and be accepted goes unfulfilled, it is difficult for us to develop trust and self-respect and to gain competence. When young people are constantly criticized and rarely praised, they are left with a legacy of self-doubt and seriously impaired social skills.

Their alienation becomes a breeding ground for future resentment and distrust. The anger is loud and clear when rebellious youth protest: "No one cares! Why should I?" "Getting even is the best revenge." Or "Don't trust anyone in authority!"

In adulthood, this alienation appears in several guises.

Self-Alienation

Low self-esteem is a sign of self-alienation in less resilient personalities, while self-delusion is an inflated overcompensation in more rebellious types. When someone flips back and forth between these two extremes, the result is identity confusion.

Low Self-Esteem

Positive affirmation and confirmation rarely played a part in the experiences of those people who still suffer recurring memories of cruel criticism from parents who refused to listen and made little attempt to understand them. Especially when there seems little certainty or security in the present, more damaged individuals may experience panic attacks and acute anxiety whenever something happens to trigger some memory of physical or emotional abuse that still haunts them, often for a lifetime. Omnipresent are distrust and fear, anger and hate, and self-loathing.

Riddled with insecurity, these vulnerable souls fear conflict, yet often unwittingly court it. When someone challenges them, they automatically go on the defensive. In their life experience, disagreement has not been a rational discussion of differences or an attempt to understand another's point of view. Somewhere the premise that it is acceptable for people to agree to disagree has been erased from consciousness, and thus they find problem-solving difficult.

When their self-loathing surfaces, a strong denial system becomes essential for their emotional survival. However, at times of undue stress, such defensive tactics often fail to adequately protect them. I sometimes use the analogy of a thick slab of mozzarella cheese to describe chronic denial. It stays firmly in place until something of major import happens, and then denial thins out to a sliver that can no longer shelter the fragile ego. That's when a mixture of self-loathing and disgust spring up to consciousness. At such times, some people may experience mini-psychotic breakdowns during which they suffer unbearable fears that sometimes erupt in the form of rage. Their whole self-image is threatened from within.

Survival, not integrity, is of paramount concern when reality cannot be distinguished from illusion.

Self-Inflation: My Way or the Highway!

Cocky arrogance signals self-delusions of superiority or grandiosity. Yet overly confident people are often mistrustful of others and remain distant and aloof. They vehemently protect their version of reality by denying any Shadow aspects that might shatter their illusions. They protect themselves from negative feedback by projecting blame onto innocent others. This form of self-deception, denying a Shadow aspect in oneself and attributing it to another, is honesty letting itself off the hook.

Over the past three decades of clinical practice, I have seen this projective tactic ruthlessly used in families where one partner is guilty of some loss of integrity, be it an infidelity, a crippling addiction, or corrupt business practices. Projection of blame can be used to twist around someone else's reality.

Graham, as we shall learn, is adept at using this tactic. Prior to a meeting in my office, his wife, Moira, phones to let me know her suspicions that her husband might be involved in some fraudulent dealings at his law firm. As yet, she has not confronted him directly.

Moira appears brittle as she sits bolt upright on the edge of her chair, as if poised for flight.

"Could you tell me about the problems you're experiencing in your marriage?" I begin.

"We used to fight all the time – about who is right," Moira explains. "My husband always says he is right. Now we barely talk!"

I turn to Graham, a distinguished-looking man in his late forties. "Is your wife correct? Do you always have to be right?"

"Well, yes," he replies, "because I always am right! I seek the truth at all times. I *know* that I'm right!"

I pause, then ask, "Is it possible by any chance for you two folks to agree to disagree?"

It's as though a puzzled mask shifts across Graham's face. He abruptly changes the subject. "Moira fabricates events, you know, especially this past year!" he nervously blurts out. "I'm convinced that she's paranoid. It's obvious that she doesn't trust me, and her endless questions about my work are driving me to distraction!"

He cautiously seeks support from me. "I know she has been talking to some of my colleagues. Is it any wonder that I don't tell her anything?"

Graham's resolute claim that he knows the "truth" suggests finality, like words carved in stone. When I ask about his capacity to "agree to disagree," to acknowledge that two people could both be right, he immediately suggests that his wife is the one with problems. He has convinced himself that it is *she* who fabricates his wrongdoings, not the other way around as Moira believes.

Graham has a hard time knowing what's wrong with this picture. In a later session he is able to admit that he has begun to notice that others' value systems are strangely at cross-purposes to his – that perhaps "something isn't right" with his perception of reality. Slowly he is gaining some insight.

Identity Confusion: The Protective Mask

A good self-awareness question to ask ourselves is: "Who am I as a person, separate and different from what I do for a living?" Without a clear knowledge of the true Self, that part of the psyche that "just is," chances are that we've invested too much energy developing a "doing-and-performing" persona – the carefully crafted image that individuals wish to present to the world at large.

The persona mask serves to shield its wearer from experiencing daunting feelings of inadequacy or embarrassment. To ward off possible rejection, the individual adopts a guise to win elusive approval and admiration from others.

Many workaholics, for example, wear the public mask of professional success, yet their personal lives are a mess. There's often a Jekyll and Hyde struggle going on within that surfaces in a real fear of intimacy and possible exposure. An expression I sometimes hear in my office goes like this: "If I let others get too close, they'll find out what I'm really like."

Frank, the man who had trouble identifying someone in his life who had integrity, was working on his own capacity for intimacy. He asked me one day if I would read what he'd written about the masks he wears, in response to a question in a workshop he had recently attended. He had chosen four masks to describe himself.

"I wear the mask of a friend. I will always give of myself." A pleaser-type Mr Nice Guy, Frank "helped" people by problem-solving for them in any way he could. The thought of a reciprocal friendship in which he would be on the receiving end of others' help was an uncomfortable concept. He needed to always stay in charge.

"I've worn the rebel mask, but I see now the dangers it presents, especially around people I want to impress – my children, employees, and friends. I profess that being a rebel is part of my reputation, though it's not been part of my self-image."

While taking Frank's history, I began to suspect that his emotional development had been arrested at the critical stage of teen-aged rebellion. It appeared that something traumatic had occurred at that time.

Around the age of puberty, the need for independence asserts itself, and adolescents start to rebel against the authority of their parents. They find fault and test rules. They're trying to find out who they are, different and separate from their role models, especially with the same-sex parent. This process, called individuation, is a necessary precursor to maturity.

At ten years of age, Frank had a lively, captivating teacher whom he adored. But one day this man started to fondle both the boys and girls in the classroom and insisted that this behaviour be kept as their "secret." The teacher was suddenly removed, gone from Frank's life without explanation. The situation was never discussed at home, as Frank's parents were reported to be preoccupied with work and had little emotional energy left for their large brood.

From then on, Frank no longer trusted authority figures. Not surprisingly, independence became a necessity.

Frank doesn't recall that this episode affected him much, one way or another. However, in our previous conversations, I had noted that he blocked out large parts of his childhood.

When I queried whether Frank might still be stuck in the "rebel" stage, he did recall a number of unconventional actions he took. He quit university in the middle of his first year, moved across the country to a big city, and while working in a factory there, kept getting better jobs. Still, a restless dissatisfaction drove him to move to several more cities.

Eventually, Frank returned home and enrolled again in university. His wilful attitude persisted, however, as he only attended the classes in subjects that were useful to his career and barely did the other course work. In his last set of finals, the professor handed out his exam form and threatened to give Frank zero if he didn't get his assignments in by eight the next morning. Frank stayed up all night and, like Tom Sawyer, got his buddies to help.

Although he escaped failure by completing his assignments, his self-esteem was not enhanced because he couldn't own the mark he received. To this day, Frank still rails against doing what is expected of him. For the most part, he only does what he wants to do.

"*I wear the chameleon mask*, never making a concrete stand. I don't often see black and white in a new area because I lack intelligence and wisdom." Frank confesses that he is too easily swayed by others' thinking on subject matter that isn't of immediate value to his career.

"*I wear the mask of confidence.* I forge forward, steamrolling to gain ground, using any means to justify the end."

Not surprisingly, Frank professes that his confidence sometimes feels phony. He still plays the teenaged rebel role even though he's married with several children. Although he has always provided well for his family, he continues to do irresponsible things at home that anger his wife and belie his expressed commitment to her.

Frank says he "lets" Julia be in charge of the children – in fact, he often can't remember where they are supposed to be or when he promised to pick them up from their activities.

Julia, on her part, is no longer willing to sacrifice her integrity by remaining a victim of his emotional neglect and irresponsible behaviour.

Self-alienation typically leads to a self-fulfilling prophecy where what a person most fears happens. Frank is risking his wife's rejection and, as a consequence, is courting the very emotional abandonment he dreads.

His corrective conscience works best when it suits him, and that is usually when he is bent on "looking good" to his colleagues. No wonder Frank's views on integrity have become so jaded.

A Prejudicial Bias

Prejudice and intolerance are forms of alienation that can be major roadblocks to the evolution of integrity.

The most obvious and insidious forms of prejudice concern a dislike or irrational hatred for those people who differ from us in race, colour, religious creed, or station in life. Most of us have heard another person utter a racial slur, the "We don't associate with *those* people," type of remark.

Hugh, an Irish-Catholic contractor, told me about a dinner party he attended when another guest he identified as a WASP individual said: "The Catholic church was built on guilt." Hugh immediately started to boil and rose to the bait. He seemed quite proud of his scathing retort, which really was itself a character assassination of the prejudiced speaker.

Beaming, Hugh chuckled over this tit-for-tat exchange: "You could have cut the atmosphere with a knife after that!" He was not yet ready to acknowledge that two wrongs don't make a right!

A more subtle but equally damaging form of prejudice comes about simply because someone we are dealing with has a personality type unlike our own. Since we don't appreciate his strengths, we tend to revile his "weaknesses." His language and behaviour clash with our particular version of what is "proper." There is bound to be tension present whenever there are personality differences.

A little knowledge *is* therefore a dangerous thing! If our appreciation of individual differences hasn't been developed, our fixed opinions are likely to remain subjectively narrow, rather than objective and universal. Limited belief systems generally stay closed to new information.

Prejudicial thinking can be as simple as convincing ourselves that Thinking-type people are smarter than Feeling-types.

Esther is a strong Thinking-type accountant who believes that everyone else should be logical and rational. Her dogmatic truths are delivered with a certainty and authority that welcome no challenge.

This boss thinks that Feeling-type people are wimps – weak, silly, and impractical. She can't understand why certain members of her staff seem so easily hurt. Esther runs a tight ship! Over the years she's taken advantage of the good-hearted loyalty of these sensitive types, gradually siphoning off much of her own work to them. This brand of prejudice is not acquainted with fairness.

Thinkers and Feelers place different emphases on certain values, and each uses a vocabulary that reflects this. Consequently, misinterpretations and misunderstandings commonly occur in their conversations.

Lydia, a warm and generous Feeling-type, is Esther's secretary. She compliments Mildred, a co-worker, for an act of kindness, saying, "That's wonderful that you've called Jesse every day since her husband died. You're such a thoughtful person!" In making this evaluation, it seems pretty clear that Lydia's primary focus is on the relationship between Mildred and Jesse.

Esther, on the other hand, utters a cryptic "Good work!" Her more impersonal comment focuses on the action that has been taken, not on Mildred's goodness.

If each individual is intolerant of the other's natural gifts of expression, then hurt feelings or angry rebuttals may be the order of the day. Esther might ridicule Lydia for what she considers false and gushy sentiment. In turn, Lydia may only hear the blunt, sharp delivery that her boss uses and miss the implied compliment.

Esther is prone to criticize and lecture people about what they should or shouldn't do. Her staff can be intimidated by her fluctuating moods – explosive outbursts or punishing silences. Such a judgmental climate is not conducive to the understanding attitudes that foster integrity.

FAMILY LEGACIES AND CRAZY-MAKING RULES

The lessons of childhood leave a lasting imprint on the psyche. If a moral sense is a natural instinct in a child, as James Wilson suggests (ix), why do so many adults fail to become morally ethical citizens?

A study into the communication patterns of dysfunctional families offers some answers. In *Co-Dependency: An Emerging Issue,* Robert Subby and John Friels describe nine oppressive "rules" that such families impose on their children. Five of them – secrecy, repression, manipulation, cynicism, and perfectionism – adversely affect the development of integrity.

Secrecy

Children are taught that it is not okay to talk about problems. Truthtelling is not high on the list of authoritarian parents who make the decisions about what can and cannot be discussed. Their "private" issues are definitely off limits.

For integrity to flourish, each family member needs to have the necessary information to know *both* sides of an issue, the full story. Otherwise, honesty becomes a meaningless concept of half-truths.

"Exactly what *is* going on here?" a child wonders. In a family climate where secrecy prevails, determining the reason for the awful silence at the dinner table titillates an anxious curiosity. Forced into second-guessing, children silently write dark and fearful scripts. Such wild guesses rarely uncover the real truth, and their mistrustful anxiety becomes chronic.

In this repressed environment, honesty is definitely *not* the best policy. In some cases there actually is some "family secret" that remains clearly out of bounds, not open for discussion. Father may be an alcoholic, but the subject is never mentioned. He eventually gets fired from his job but continues to go off somewhere every morning as if nothing has happened.

There is no model for good listening skills when parents silence complaints or neglect to comment on poor behaviour. These children tragically have no one to talk to when things go wrong. They are left to feel "bad" for having problems.

When their personal rights and freedom of expression are not respected or honoured, years of repressed anger and guilt build up a reservoir of resentment that undermines self-esteem. The competence they might have gained from problem-solving and working things through with an understanding parent is denied to these children.

When a rebellious child dares to question what is really going on, such independent thought is discouraged by a response of hysterical outrage or prolonged, deafening silence. However, the repressed defiance lingers on, and sooner or later these rebels will defy convention – a recipe for lost integrity at some future date.

Severe panic attacks brought Sharon into my office. She described her family this way: "My father was a business tycoon who dominated my mother, and us kids never brought up problems because we were all afraid of my mercurial father. Lately I've been getting into unexpected rages myself, but I'm not sure why. The other day my husband told me to shut up about my problems, and I just went ballistic!"

"I can be quite merciless," Sharon confides. "Last week Jack refused to go to my favourite charity ball. I was so angry that I told him he was nothing but a selfish pig – too fat to squeeze into his tuxedo!"

After making this nasty remark, it was some time before she spoke to her husband. Jack was being punished for thwarting Sharon's plans. Her own outrageous outburst hadn't happened – a lesson she had learned at home. "I used to be good at blocking bad things out, but lately this isn't working. I'm terrified I'm becoming just like my father."

There's no integrity in ridiculing others, especially around their Achilles heel. Being overweight was Jack's worst nightmare because staying youthful was his vain preoccupation. He kept himself in shape despite a yearning for chocolate whenever he was stressed out. Not being able to anticipate Sharon's frequent outbursts kept him always on edge, so staying slim was no mean feat.

Ironically, Sharon had married someone who shared little. "A penny for your thoughts!" was her favourite saying. The distancing tactics and tit-for-tat revenge they had learned in childhood had become a pattern for this unfortunate couple. Their efforts to find a mutually agreeable solution rarely worked.

Repression

The family does not believe that feelings should be expressed openly. Inhibited parents who find both angry outbursts and gushy sentiment equally uncomfortable discourage honest expression of emotions. Unhappiness instead gets expressed internally in passive-aggressive responses. Children seethe and sulk, fall into moods, and retreat into silent victimhood.

Self-control cannot develop unless we are first free to express the full range of human emotions. The matter of discerning what is socially acceptable and what is not must be learned through experience.

Denial plays a major role in repression. Parents who repress their own negative feelings also tend to remain unaware of the negative emotions of sorrow, pain, fear, anger, guilt, or shame in their children. These parents tend to remain stoic or fatalistic when things don't go as planned, and regularly admonish their children to "Keep a stiff upper lip!" or "Pull up your socks!"

Problems arise when a parent's *disowned* frustration flares up and gets projected outwards. The child who is blamed unfairly is left filled with anxiety while, paradoxically, the parent who is safely released from his or her own anger remains relatively calm.

Subsequent discussion of the problem is rarely encouraged because the situation is "over and done with," supposedly forgotten. Not surprisingly, fairness and justice remain fuzzy concepts.

A false independence is fostered because children are *expected* to handle their own problems and thereby make their parents proud. When children in pain receive no emotional support, they feel abandoned and devalued. Their helplessness, loneliness, and despair work together to destroy their self-confidence. Introverted children are at special risk, because they often lack the confidence to seek experiences outside the family that might help bolster their self-esteem.

Integrity is a foreign concept in these unhappy circumstances. Kevin, who grew up in such a repressed environment, is having difficulty letting his wife know what he is going through at work. "My whole family was passive-aggressive!" he exclaims. "Whoever was the most sneaky and quiet got the prize for the best kid. It got so we never dared express any feelings. I never knew whether I was angry or they were. I know I tried to figure out exactly what did happen so that I could avoid it the next time. There was never a time I remember my parents sitting down with me to discuss why I was so upset."

Then he adds: "If depression is about repressed anger and feelings of helplessness, then it's no wonder I battle with black moods all the time. When I'm gone, I'm gone for a long time. Poor Molly doesn't know what's going on and I don't either – I'm completely incommunicado!"

Silent withdrawal prohibits resolution, so a lot of unfinished business never gets addressed. No wonder this couple is having problems around trust and honesty.

Manipulation

Communication between family members is usually indirect, with one person acting as the messenger between two others.

Triangles form in families when one member talks to another about a third member who is causing problems or is not present. For example, children often go to Mother because she's readily available to talk about or send messages to Dad, or to complain about a sibling. This pragmatic, indirect communication creates an atmosphere of mistrust. The family motto could be: "Whatever works, use it!"

Unwittingly, manipulative children become good strategists who enjoy competitive one-upmanship. Their habit of talking *about* other people instead of *to* them slips into careless gossip. There's a game-like quality to such exchanges that can be seductive.

Integrity quickly evaporates in the face of a temptation to exaggerate, falsify, or otherwise distort messages because the other party is not there to confront any errors or omissions.

Children typically test limits by trying to play off Mom against Dad. If they don't like the answer one parent gives, they will ask the other one if they can go somewhere or do something, get such-and-such, or sleep over at a friend's house. Such manipulations only work if parents have neglected their own relationship and communication between them is poor. When a child's double-dealing is exposed, too often duped parents get angry with each other and neglect to reprimand the child.

These scrambled communication links, once established, create enmeshed family systems in which each member's ego boundaries are hopelessly blurred. It's difficult to know where one person's responsibility stops and another's begins. No one respects anybody's right to be spoken to directly. Paranoia prevails when truth can't be tested at the source.

Similar manipulations get played out in the larger arena, at school and with friends. Learning how to trick the teacher into blaming someone else for one's unruly behaviour stirs up excitement. It can soon become second nature to tell tales that impress but mislead others.

Carole, an articulate writer, is clearly having trouble respecting ego boundaries. She has a bad habit of being invasive and not minding her own business, especially when her husband is on the phone.

"I'm having trouble 'minding my onions' when Dick gets upset because he's just had an argument with his sister on the phone," she admits. "I can tell he's fuming. In no time at all, I'm in a mood. It doesn't take long until I find myself thoroughly involved. I'm sounding off about how he should have handled his sister, and just out of the blue, I find myself becoming vindictive. It's *his* fault that I got into a mood!"

She pauses. "Most of the time we end up in an awful row about some inane thing totally unrelated to what was going on. We'll destroy each other if we keep going on like this. When am I ever going to learn to stop interfering? He needs to be respected for his efforts, not micro-managed."

Carol is gradually learning to stay objective but interested. She no longer jumps in to "fix" other people's problems.

Cynicism

Children are told: "Do as I say and not as I do." The modelling that takes place when parents rationalize their own misdemeanours has a profound effect on young minds. Children learn to mimic this duplicity or to mistrust the word of others.

While a father is teaching his sixteen-year-old son to drive, he bawls him out for exceeding the sixty-kilometre limit. A week later, the family is on a road trip, and Joey pipes up: "Dad, for Pete's sake, you're going 140! You told me the speed limit's 100."

His father's answer avoids the real issue. "When you're a man, you'll be able to exercise your own judgment about such things."

Advice and action don't jibe. Dad's self-righteous explanation is an attempt to make himself look good no matter what is going on. No wonder Joey is growing up cynical.

Such mixed messages discourage honest discussion. Smart-alecky people who push the rules are the ones most apt to complain about other rule-breakers. For themselves, they find "exceptions to every rule."

Laziness plays a part in the practice of saying one thing and then doing another. If we tell one lie, it's easier to continue the fabrication than to take responsibility for the discrepancy.

Some call their avoidance of the truth "diplomacy"; others rationalize that it's "kindness"; still others label it "simple pragmatism." Whatever label it goes by – a fib, falsehood, or deception – a lie is still a lie.

Perfectionism

Children get the message that they should be strong, good, right, and perfect. In families where perfectionism and idealism reign, it often doesn't pay to admit mistakes or failures. Children in these families learn early that they are expected to enhance the family or a parent's reputation by doing well at school and having a successful career. These are the over-achievers, the "good kids" who become overly responsible adults.

In such families, standards are set exceedingly high, the competitive spirit is greatly admired, and only excellence brings praise. Winning is the ultimate goal, so any errors are scorned, and failure is the ultimate shame. Children accordingly fret over their mistakes if they've let their parents down. The child subsequently feels like a "bad" person. It's a double whammy if this disgrace brings a temporary or prolonged withdrawal of parental approval.

Soon such pressured children cannot love an "imperfect" Self. When things don't go as planned, their self-criticism overwhelms their self-nurturing capacity. It's little wonder that they find dishonesty such a temptation. Rationalizing or blaming others for their mistakes becomes a seductive habit.

When their self-esteem depends on external accolades, children are taught to validate their own strengths and see their positive image through the eyes of others. In other words, their self-image is based on an external frame of reference or projection.

Of course, the reverse is true. This dynamic also feeds a false arrogance that unconsciously disowns and projects its own weaknesses, doubts, and fears, and recognizes them as existing in others. Perfectionists readily judge others but fail to own the whole Self, warts and all – a prerequisite for integrity. In the dark places of the psyche, a false reality becomes the only truth. Anxiety can threaten to dismantle this dangerous house of cards at any time. Perfectionism demands that all the variables in a situation be under one's control, so power and control become extremely important.

There's great wisdom in the idea that we can't fix something until we recognize that it is broken. In recognizing that something went wrong during our moral development to adversely affect our character development, we take the first step.

Now, we'll look at why perfectionists become increasingly obsessive and why obsessions and compulsions are likely to topple our integrity. Perfectionism is not necessarily a trait that should be admired; in fact it can become a curse.

5

Obsession: A Major Threat
to Integrity

Unfortunately, the sort of individual who is programmed to ignore
personal distress and keep pushing for the top is frequently programmed
to disregard signs of grave and imminent danger as well.

Jon Krakauer, *Into Thin Air*

OBSESSION AND INTEGRITY

If I had to make an educated guess about who might eventually lose
his or her integrity, it would likely be an individual who has become
obsessively fixated on a thought, idea, or action. It's not easy to
make intelligent *and* wise moral and ethical decisions when everything else is swept aside to accommodate some narrowly focused
pursuit, especially when it becomes an irrational one. When nothing else matters to us except getting to some sought-after goal, the
excessive efforts required can be exhilarating but thoroughly
destabilizing. This driving force to rush from Plan A to goal B could
be labelled a "fixation on B."

This chapter's epigraph comes from Jon Krakauer's horrendous
story of the spring of 1996 when twelve men and women died
attempting to climb Mount Everest. Krakauer was part of it all.
Some time elapsed before he sufficiently recovered from his own
ordeal to gain enough objectivity to write about it.

Krakauer describes the levels of misery and peril that all the members of his group were suffering by late in the expedition which would
have sent more balanced individuals packing for home long before
reaching that stage. He describes the expedition's leader, Rob Hall, as
a "compulsively methodical man" who had elaborate systems in place
to ensure safety. "To get this far one had to have an uncommonly

obdurate personality ... in order to succeed you must be exceedingly driven, but if you're too driven you're likely to die" (233).

The tragedy on the mountain revealed the worst and the best in the climbers. Acts of reckless greed driven by vain ambition, by cruel disdain for others in peril, and by heartbreaking decisions to abandon injured and exhausted climbers to die alone were offset by lofty acts of heroism. Some made remarkable efforts to find lost climbers, to save the dying. Tragically, above 26,000 feet, with oxygen thin and a storm threatening, "the line between zeal and reckless summit fever becomes grievously thin. Thus the slopes of Everest are littered with corpses" (ibid.).

While most earthbound people will never have the inclination, money, or opportunity to make such a climb, obsessive types can readily commiserate because they are similarly driven, albeit towards somewhat less spectacular strivings.

WHAT'S THE DIFFERENCE BETWEEN AN OBSESSION AND A COMPULSION?

An obsession is "an idea, emotion or impulse that repetitively and insistently forces itself into consciousness even though it is unwelcome" (Campbell, *Psychiatric Dictionary*, 423).

There's little for us to worry about if some obsessional thought or idea is short lived and doesn't unduly interfere with our decision-making functions. Usually we can remain in control and minimize its impact by diverting our attention safely on to other topics. In other words, the obsession doesn't end up running us.

A compulsion is an unwanted need that rises into consciousness and compels the individual to perform some repetitive act.

A compulsion is fuelled by the same fears that generate an obsessive thought or emotion. If the compulsive person fails to perform a ritualistic act that is intended to block out such fears, anxiety only increases, and the noxious thoughts persist.

In the early stages of obsession, people make cognitive decisions on impulse simply to ease the ubiquitous self-doubt that haunts them. Through a single-minded form of intellectualizing, they avoid the necessity of having to confront the emotional side of an issue. Similarly, they are able to disown uncomfortable feelings of being submissive or weak.

When their obsessive thinking persists over time and they can no longer consciously control their thoughts, many develop a complicated array of "shoulds" and "oughts" that get incorporated into a series of rigid and sometimes ritualistic rules. These mantras substitute for the more normal "sense of duty" that people with integrity possess. Those with blind ambition make up their own rules as they fixate on some seductive goal and expect others to follow.

Some obsessive people become preoccupied with emotional survival. Overly cautious in their efforts to regain an illusion of self-control, they attempt to manipulate ever more variables in their lives. Some eventually refuse to take any monetary, business, or social risks because such trial-and-error experimentation might lead to grievous mistakes.

These frightened souls pay little attention to the impact of their actions on others. They seek security by choosing the familiar and known, safe thing to do. An obsessive man called Charlie often distorted others' words because of his growing paranoia, complaining that he had been "offended once too often." He limited social outings with his wife to dinner at one neighbourhood restaurant where the maitre d' made a fuss over him, or to a show at a nearby movie theatre. The isolated couple's world became smaller and smaller. By making these and other restrictive decisions, Charlie showed no sympathy for his depressed wife's plaintive protests, "We never see any of our old friends anymore!"

When such compulsive acts fail to ease their sometimes unbearable distress, these troubled folks find their obsessional thought patterns growing more negative and convoluted. No longer in touch with their own normal needs and wishes, they develop harsh black-and-white attitudes towards duty and morality. Haunted by dominance and submissive issues, they experience an emotional remoteness from others that can lead them to suffer a sense of alienated resentment.

I often ask my obsessional clients a variation on the question "Why do you think you've chosen to 'hang your hat' on that particular hook right now?" In other words, why is that special thought or idea demanding so much of their attention?

Sometimes the fixation is an obsession with work, or it may be neatness, cleanliness, high marks, or the perfect relationship – the list goes on. Usually it turns out that this particular focus is symptomatic of some unresolved emotional issue that threatens to erupt if the illusion of controlled omnipotence is lost. In actual fact, whatever the obsession, it has likely served these people all too well. Their singularly narrow preoccupation has left them locked into their defences, totally self-absorbed, and thus personally irresponsible. They have seemingly little natural curiosity about why they needed the obsession in the first place. Yet without this self-knowledge and insight, they cannot begin the work of rebuilding lost integrity.

Full-blown obsession is best described as "inner chaos." From there it is a long and difficult journey to recover one's sanity – to gradually learn to think in a normal fashion and feel peaceful again.

CHAOS THEORY

Chaos, of course, is the pole opposite of order. Chaos theory addresses the apparently random behaviour that occurs within a deterministic system such as the weather. The theory goes like this: "The unpredictability of a chaotic system is not due to any lack of governing laws but to the outcome being sensitive to minute, unmeasurable variations in the initial condition" (Honderich, 129).

In human terms, our personality is shaped by hereditary predispositions to certain traits. Our character, on the other hand, is strongly influenced by a variety of spontaneous responses to a determinative system of rewards and punishments. From the day we are born, a multitude of seemingly innocuous but often surprising or disturbing influences can strongly tip the delicate balance between the polarities that help determine our character, sometimes forever. For example, the separation of parents, especially during a child's formative years, can turn that child's innocent trust into its polar opposite: a sceptical, suspicious nature. Thereafter, issues around trust, security, and intimacy will likely challenge the person and be an ever-present source of anxiety.

Often it is difficult to know exactly what has gone wrong. Melody is an idealistic teenager who has set her sights high. Her career path and goals seem admirable. In high school this bright, ambitious student has learned to practise fair dealings and use ethical guidelines to steer a straight course for herself. She exercises self-control, considers the impact of her actions on others, and weighs the short-term and long-term consequences of her decisions. So far, so good. Her integrity seems to be developing as it should.

Along the way, however, this idealistic picture changes. As chaos theory reminds us, the unpredictable outcome that leads to chaos may simply be a sensitivity to something like her misguided ambition of perfectionism – certainly an immeasurable and unpredictable variation in the early stages of developmental growth. By insisting that she do *everything* perfectly, Melody sets unrealistic goals for herself. Whenever she falls short of these expectations, she grows increasingly despondent and eventually slips into a clinical depression.

PERFECTIONISM: A SIGN OF OBSESSION

Perfectionism is a disposition to regard anything short of perfection as absolutely unacceptable.

Why would perfectionists, of all people, lose their integrity? Many see perfectionism as an admirable trait, not a crippling character flaw. In fact, obsession is a sign of perfectionism. The greater the level of perfectionism, the more obsessive the person will become.

Let's look at some of perfectionism's attributes, the ones most likely to contribute to the loss of integrity.

Special Treatment

Perfectionists believe, or are made to believe, that they are highly intelligent, even superior beings capable of special excellence or mastery. Their achievements reflect a single-minded ambition to be the best at whatever they choose to do. Many of our politicians, entertainers, accomplished athletes, and leading scientists are professionally successful, although their personal lives are a mess. They live their lives full out, but not wisely.

This idea of "specialness" can foster a dangerous arrogance or "entitlement" attitudes that revel in being an "exception to the rule," someone exempt from community standards and regulations. Full-blown arrogance even considers itself "above the law."

Self-Doubt

Perfectionists require and demand external admiration to ward off their repressed self-doubt. Underneath what appears to be a self-confident, self-sufficient, and often cocky facade lurks a surprising insecurity, left over from a childhood where acceptance was conditionally based on performance evaluation. Typically, the parents reserved their praise and rewards for times when the child exceeded expectations.

The Feeling-Being side of the personality, the Self, was rarely rewarded. No one thought to remark that a child had spoken with sensitivity or made a thoughtful gesture at a difficult moment. No one seemed to notice that a child had a wonderful capacity for warmth and generosity, for making and keeping friends.

When external standards or expectations are raised too high, these "good kids" just try harder. Below an earnest exterior, however, they frequently hide nagging fears of imminent failure. To ward off such a fate, perfectionists tend to deny their shortcomings or errors and keep their faults or mistakes secret. Neglecting to tell the truth is their form of lying – all in all, a poor environment in which to develop integrity's core value of honesty. Not surprisingly, perfectionists periodically experience an inner emptiness and despair, a feeling of being "a phony."

Greedy Ambition

Obsessives learn early on that sharpening any skills that guarantee external praise is a worthwhile pursuit. Their anxious need for positive recognition thus becomes a driving force. But reaching one goal is never enough to build up their confidence, so another, more ambitious one must be sought. More is always better!

Later on, it may be their standard of living that needs upgrading. A lifestyle is an impressive way to reassure oneself. Unfortunately, the compulsive pursuit of richer material trappings rarely satisfies for long. Cravings cannot produce self-acceptance.

Denial and Self-Loathing

Perfectionists proudly take ownership of their positive traits but largely disown their weaknesses. If things do start to go badly, however, their strong defence mechanisms become useful allies in protecting their idealized image. Favourites here include denying wrongdoing, employing half-truths, and projecting unwanted faults onto innocent others.

But too many dreaded failures force up to consciousness the self-loathing that underlies arrogance. At such times of angst, the acute distress the approval-seekers experience makes them recklessly impulsive. Their frantic efforts to convince others of the legitimacy and "rightness" of their claims only intensify. Manipulation and deception become necessary tactics when the ego is so fragile.

Blind Ambition

When ambition's heady goals take top priority, everyday responsibilities become a burden. Consequently, many hard-drivers gradually let slip the niceties of life, the admirable traits of politeness, consideration, punctuality, reliability, and loyalty. As they are caught up in a hurry-hurry, rush-rush drive to impress and outperform others, their attentions narrow and stay riveted to some chosen course. The competition must be conquered, bottom-line costs lowered, and efficiency kept ever higher, no matter the personal cost or the sacrifice demanded of others. "This isn't a popularity contest," the perfectionist rationalizes.

If the perfectionist is a stay-at-home parent, she may tie herself and her kids up in knots. She can't ever relax because she perceives her household tasks to be endless. If her children procrastinate over their duties, she explodes and berates them. Then guilt sets in, and she does the job for them. Mixed messages are everywhere.

She teaches what was taught to her: accomplishment is everything. Memories of shame linger for a lifetime, her mother's admonitions still ringing in her ear: "Those marks aren't good enough. You're made of better stuff!" Both parties possess a measuring yardstick that is set unrealistically high. Rest and relaxation don't come easily to these harried souls, parents and children alike.

Loss of the Authentic Self

The achievement of singular ambitions counts for little if we lose our authentic Self. This is surely one of the great tragedies of lost integrity.

To believe that you *are* your persona, how you wish to be seen . publicly by others, can only work so long. The American painter Gerald Murphy found this out after his son became seriously ill. He stopped painting and suffered profound unease because of an uncertain reality about who he was.

In *Everybody Was So Young* Amanda Vaill sums up Murphy's dilemma: "As a young man he had been haunted by feelings of otherness, of difference, either social, or sexual, or personal." He apparently fled America for Europe to seek a world that wouldn't hold him to standards that would find him wanting. Now this tragic turn of events changed everything: "His creations – his paintings, his marriage, the children who embodied his and Sara's fondest hopes, the 'loaded and fragrant' way of life they invented together – had all been corrupted" (224).

Like so many other perfectionists, Murphy couldn't adjust to his own less than perfect world. "What he was left with was his own uncertain nature – a nature he had never been taught to value, and which he feared would revolt the people he most cherished if it were ever revealed to them" (224).

Lost Creativity

The narrow focus that excellence requires can drive a person crazy. Brian, a perfectionistic draftsman, describes the inner turmoil that led him to contact me:

> When I get obsessive, nothing else exists for me. All else fades into oblivion. Life is on a pinhead. Everything outside and around me becomes dangerous, a threat to my survival.
>
> It's as though I'm in a metal straitjacket. As I start to get obsessive about something, I beat through the walls I build around myself to protect me from out there. As my focus narrows, I go inside – first through a glass wall, then a curtained wall. Next, I pass through a brick wall, and then when I'm really driven, an iron wall. Finally, I reach a six-inch thick wall of steel that finally protects me from chaos. It's like I'm safely encased in a bank vault.
>
> When I heard you on a radio program the first time, nothing broke through. I was oblivious. A year later, the second time I heard you interviewed, time stopped. Your voice penetrated the

wall. Physically shaken, I turned off the freeway and parked by the side of the road totally immobilized. I remember thinking, this woman is speaking to me!

Up until the second episode, Brian couldn't recognize that his obsessive behaviour was destroying his creativity. Too many of his days were unproductive because he got lost in reworking some small, relatively insignificant detail. In desperation he began taking shortcuts by neglecting to ensure the accuracy of his measurements, and as a consequence turned out some pretty shoddy work. No longer able to rush, he lost several corporate clients because of missed deadlines. Emotionally he just wasn't there. The integrity that he boasted about was disappearing.

As the old saying goes, "When the student is ready, the teacher will appear."

HOW DOES OBSESSION DISTORT CHARACTER?

The distortion of character and, therefore, of integrity occurs most often when people impulsively succumb over time to the powerful temptation to do the expedient or seductive thing. They stubbornly ignore vague warnings that ill will or bad consequences will ensue. Unwittingly, they become their own worst enemy.

Years ago while I was doing an internship at a hospital, I remember my total frustration on hearing that Betty, a deeply disturbed obsessive-compulsive patient who had been caught shoplifting, had gone to see the film *The Exorcist* on her weekend pass. At the time, I wondered why she would expose herself to further trauma.

But obsessive people do typically shift from the awareness of one idea to an oppositional view. Experience has taught them that staying with one version of reality often produces unpleasant emotions. Therefore, the expedient pain-free thing to do is to switch tactics, to proceed to say or do the opposite thing. Swinging back and forth between positions, not knowing what one really wants or doesn't want, is typical behaviour.

In group therapy, Betty typically championed healthy actions that she and the other group members could pursue. When she was left to her own devices on the weekend, however, this healthy attitude shifted. A determined wilfulness took over, and Betty's self-nurturing capacity seemingly disappeared.

PARADIGM FOR OBSESSION

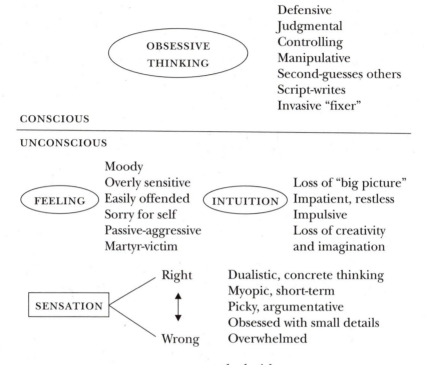

Figure 5.1 Conceptualization of an obsessional paradigm

Now we will explore the inner dynamics that occur as people become more obsessive, and examine why these changes can jeopardize our personal integrity.

OBSESSIONAL PARADIGM

Figure 5.1 is my conceptualization of an obsessional paradigm. It is based on Jung's theory of psychological types developed in the early 1920s to explain personality differences.

This paradigm attempts to show what happens inside the psyche when obsessional thoughts and compulsive acts reach the stage where they dominate the personality, first compelling, then dictating, and eventually controlling how an individual thinks and behaves.

The following explanation outlines how the functions of Thinking, Feeling, Intuition, and Sensation are adversely affected by the dynamics of obsession. Integrity is eroded whenever the dark side of these functions begins to dominate and change one's character.

Thinking

Healthy thinking is rational, logical, analytical, pragmatic, fair, and realistic. Because the Thinking function is naturally focused and goal-oriented, problem-solving is ordinarily one of its strengths. It has the capacity to analyse a problem, examine it logically and objectively, and subsequently come to some practical and sensible conclusion.

Whenever attaining a specific goal becomes a *fixation*, an end in itself, however, Thinking turns obsessional and its negative Shadow aspects start to influence decision-making. The obsessive person becomes more arrogant, sceptical, critical, and judgmental. Controlling behaviour increases, and anyone who protests risks the wrath of vindictive reprisals. These power struggles are fuelled by an overly competitive spirit bent on winning.

As obsessive thoughts overtax the Thinking function, persistent ruminations cloud meaning, purpose, and clarity. The person's range of attention narrows, and extraneous information fails to register. Thus tunnel vision typically diverts psychic energy away from larger personal concerns to safer impersonal and concrete issues.

Complex strategies and elaborate schemes are developed to restore order and confidence when reality becomes too painful.

Tim, an articling student, prepares for a law school debate by staying up most of the night plotting how he will answer every possible rebuttal he might expect to encounter. His focus is on the "scripts" he has written for the other side, not on preparing his own arguments. Consequently, he has difficulty listening objectively and without prejudice to the opposition's discussion. Second-guessing others in general reveals a lack of respect and is an indication of poor ego boundaries.

Diversionary tactics help others ease their anxiety. Their thoughts may suddenly drift off on an unrelated tangent and cause them to make inappropriate choices.

A week after her mother's death, Lucille, a librarian, pours all her energies into a whirlwind of community fund-raising that leaves her totally exhausted. She won't consider asking someone else to take her place. Consequently, she is left with limited resources to cope with the depression that the grieving process causes. By blocking out her sorrow, she cannot be emotionally present to nurture herself or her family who are suffering their own loss.

Becoming trapped in circular thinking that goes nowhere is a common problem. Like an old record stuck in a groove, Perry, a systems analyst, endlessly ruminates over every last detail of the days before his wife "suddenly" left him. He says he has no idea why she did this.

A temporary puff of optimism pushes him to volunteer to organize the office Christmas party. He desperately wants others to see him in a good light, even though he feels overwhelmed and is barely functioning at work. He has told no one of his plight, so he will have to dream up some excuse for why his wife is not at the party. One lie will soon beget another.

There's no integrity in deluding oneself to impress others.

Unwanted negative thoughts and feelings are disowned and projected outwards. Closeness and intimacy require a commitment that severely obsessive individuals can no longer make. Rather than risk rejection, they do and say foolish and often cruel things that provoke an angry response, thereby inducing the rejection they most fear – a self-fulfilling prophecy.

One night in an explosive fury Jamal, a meticulous craftsman, told his wife, Christa, that he couldn't stand her anymore. Needless to say, she was devastated. Jamal had been emotionally withdrawn for some time, but she still catered to his every need. Unwittingly, she was sacrificing her own emotional health in fruitless efforts to salvage their relationship, all by herself.

Once this couple understood that the dynamics of obsession produce personality changes that negatively influence the way a person thinks and acts, Jamal was able to recognize that it was his own self-loathing he was projecting onto Christa. She had refused to be sexual with him because of his emotional neglect. In turn, he was punishing her for what he believed was *her* rejection of him.

Christa had lost her objectivity, and her own clear sense of Self. She didn't stop to ask if Jamal's accusations and pronouncements were actually true. Did she need to take his irrational behaviour personally? Whose problem was it anyway? Why was she not trying to change her own reactions? And lastly, what was she avoiding by not taking full responsibility for her own welfare and happiness?

All of obsession's forms of "busy work" only temporarily relieve anxiety. Soon there are no reserves left to draw on, only exhaustion and dark thoughts.

Integrity is never served well by faulty judgments, partly because relentless thoughts have a bad habit of running over and discounting Feeling's more humane and gentle nature. This is unfortunate, because integrity is nurtured by the Feeling function.

FEELING

Feeling is the watchdog of ethical values, because the Feeling function makes its decisions based on what it values and appreciates. It focuses on relationships and how others are affected by our actions. The health of integrity in a society therefore depends on how other-directed and compassionate its citizens are towards those less fortunate. The moody, overly sensitive dark side of Feeling that takes everything personally is too self-absorbed to care.

Such disinterest affects the application of rules and regulations. Negative Feeling fails to be flexible enough to take into consideration realities such as context, safety, and the health and welfare of all concerned.

Positive Feeling in general loses by default when obsessional Thinking dominates the personality. The empathy and compassion necessary for integrity go missing when the compulsive need to re-check details, make long, involved lists, or rework countless drafts drains the psyche of all its positive energy. The body signals its distress, but obsessive people have little awareness of their churning stomachs or taut shoulder muscles. Until these warning signs become conscious, they cannot take any corrective measures.

Intensity replaces Feeling's playful and mischievious attitude. They consider taking time out to show sensitivity and express caring thoughts a costly waste of precious time. Self-nurturing activities also take a back seat.

These people stifle conciliatory actions because that would be considered an "unwise" sign of weakness, of backing down. Consequently, the problems persist. No wonder the deeply felt emotions that foster the feeling values of integrity are repressed into numbness or extinguished altogether.

Such blocked feelings are experienced as sullen moods and stewing resentments that fester just below the surface of consciousness, ever ready to erupt. Even simple frustrations produce extreme negativity.

Jaws set, obsessive people glare or stare coldly. Some withdraw into a hostile swirl of emotions, while others tune out or leave the scene to find distractions elsewhere. Many use fatigue as an excuse to procrastinate or "forget." Their touchy over-sensitivity is a misguided form of feeling that distorts the truth. Emotionally unavailable individuals are not good at sorting out "who did what to whom." No wonder Feeling's key values grow fuzzy. Obsessive people don't know what they want or what is right. Such confusion makes it easy for them to sink into depression and despair. Panic attacks or brief claustrophobic episodes signal that Feeling's life-giving energy is being cut off.

Dangerous defence mechanisms click in. An ad in *Time* magazine advertising "RPS: A Courier System Company" shows a dog ignoring a red ball. The caption reads: if you *can't* teach the *old dog* new tricks, get a *new* dog." This is a perfect example of dissociation – pretending that people and things, no longer useful, don't exist. Pragmatism's bottom-line thinking once again tramples over unsung loyalty and genuine caring for others, without which integrity is impossible.

INTUITION

Intuition loses its big-picture vision when someone crosses the line into obsession.

Ordinarily, Intuition uses an instinctive sixth sense, or rapid cognition, to gather information in an unconscious way. Answers or solutions simply pop up whole and complete, seemingly unannounced. We experience Intuition as a "gut reaction." It is "thinking without thinking," according to Malcom Gladwell in *Blink*. An intuitive conclusion, he says, is not thought out in words, but it can be deconstructed later (45).

Intuition sees meaning and relationships in concepts, and its insights stretch beyond the concrete information that the five senses provide. Presented with an array of possibilities, Intuition can often discern probabilities that might otherwise remain invisible. Its imaginative creativity is used in brainstorming techniques.

Obsession, however, turns brainstorming into tortuous "script-writing," rehearsing endless possibilities. The "big picture" disappears as the individual is flooded with wild or improbable ideas or thoughts, some of which are distorted by paranoia. "It's like a tap that can't be turned off" is how one client describes his angst.

Positive intuition is quick, clever, curious, and wise. Negative intuition is slow, easily bored, impatient, and impulsive, and it has a tendency to be reckless.

Such chaotic processes block creativity. They dull artistic talents and spiritual inspiration, and can seriously curtail imaginative enterprises and innovative scientific discovery.

It is very frightening when a natural-born Intuitive can no longer tap into quick answers. Peter, one of my clients, a clever innovator of ideas, talked frequently about how slow he had become in grasping anything but very concrete ideas. I had to provide him with numerous specific examples or deliver my messages in story form. Often it took him weeks to figure out some abstract concept.

One day I was letting Peter in through the intercom system when he called out: "Hi, it's me – the new Pete!" He was ecstatic because he now understood the reason for his slow recovery. All week he had read and reread everything about his psychological type and now understood that he was a natural Intuitive who had lost his "big picture" vision. That's why he was having such difficulty understanding abstract ideas and theoretical models. He had become thoroughly bogged down in practicalities and endless details.

"No wonder your anxiety has been sky-high these past few years!" I exclaimed. For an inventor to lose his Intuition and his ingenuity is a catastrophe.

Such revelations occur many times in my office when a person's best function no longer works effectively. The opposite, least-well developed or inferior function must struggle with tasks that don't suit its set of skills. But more about the Inferior Function later.

The obsessive personality is clearly in deep trouble when the positive attributes of Thinking, Feeling, and Intuition are replaced by the dark side of these functions. Wise thoughts grow scarce, and a powerful negativity corrupts character development.

Sadly, Sensation suffers a similar fate.

SENSATION

Healthy sensation perceives the physical reality of people and objects through its five senses – sight, sound, taste, smell, and touch. On one level, sense impressions are made up of observable data such as the shape, size, and texture of an object. No judgment is involved when these details are registered into consciousness.

On another level, sense faculties respond physiologically, and the brain translates these sensory impressions into thoughts and feelings about the concrete image. Sensation focuses on here-and-now experiences and concrete realities. It then devises practical and pragmatic reasons to explain what is occurring or what is being done.

Obsessional thinking changes all this. As anxiety climbs, Sensation's mathematical, slow, thorough step-by-step processing of "all the trees in the forest" goes awry. These are the signs to watch for when negative Sensation is in charge.

A dualistic thinking develops which is concrete and extreme. Things are either black or white, right or wrong: there are no shades of grey. If their choice is challenged, obsessional people get defensive and become picky, petty, and argumentative. They lecture in great detail about the superiority of their idea while putting down their opponents' ideas with disdain. "You should think like I do!" is the message. Defensive Sensation distrusts words and wants concrete evidence. "Show me," or "prove it," it says.

Obsessive persons' listening is largely selective, usually focused on information that supports their point of view. More often than not, rather than listening, they will be rehearsing what to say or do next.

Short-term thinking dominates most of their conversations. They make choices based solely on the immediate practicality of a proposed action, ignoring long-term considerations for the future.

Because negative Sensation craves pleasure, addictions, sexual acting-out, and fraud become common problems. As the obsession takes over, it is no longer enough to savour simple, concrete sights and sounds, and truly appreciate just what *is*. Instead, an impulsive neediness distorts Sensation's normal sense of well-being into a voracious appetite.

Seemingly overnight, someone becomes a fanatical gourmet cook who stuffs herself to ease the nervous emptiness inside.

Another person begins smoking two packs of cigarettes a day and frequents smoky bars. A keen interest in wine can soon turn into alcoholism.

Many obsessive people develop a heightened awareness of all things sexual. Some act out their cravings by seeking younger, attractive companions, often from a lower socio-economic level, to wine and dine and bed. Many have extramarital affairs that go on for years, with promises to leave the marriage never met. A few obsessive personalities promiscuously lust after scintillating sex wherever it is available. This slippery slope of cross-addictions and excesses is reported every day in the media as people lose their hard-won integrity in dubious affairs, shady deals, and neglected health.

While excess appeals to some, others boast about their frugality. In his book, *Peter Munk: The Making of a Modern Tycoon*, Donald Rumball quotes Peter Munk, the chairman of Barrick Gold Corporation: "It's a great luxury that I don't have to think what I'm going to have for breakfast. I've had the same breakfast for 35 years. I dress the same way. I pretty well wear the same ties." Munk goes on to describe himself as a pragmatic guy with no doubts: "I know black and I know white."

Munk reports that his first wife told him he had a limited IQ, because people who are really well educated with a really high IQ know there are no blacks and whites. Munk concludes: "I don't have this problem" (347–8).

Workaholism is a special case of obsession. Because it is so prevalent in today's society, the next chapter examines this phenomenon in some depth to discover why so many workaholics lose their integrity.

6

Why Workaholics Lose Their Integrity

> A workaholic is a work-obsessed individual who becomes emotionally crippled and addicted to control and power, caught up in a compulsive drive to gain personal approval and public recognition.

It is one thing when an obsessive-prone individual develops a disconcerting compulsion to keep everything spotless and insists that other family members measure up to some arbitrary standard. The obsession with work is made doubly problematic by an added component, the addiction to power and control. Its impact on the family is already tragic, but workaholism affects a wider circle of business colleagues and the institutions where these people work.

To understand *why* and *how* these ambitious workers eventually lose their integrity, we explore three threads that weave throughout this addiction. The first looks at the etiology and who is at risk. The second examines the pattern that the breakdown follows. The third explains why recovering from this addiction and regaining integrity is no easy task.

PERFECTIONISM LEADS TO OBSESSION LEADS TO NARCISSISM

Workaholics are a relatively resilient group of survivors. These overly responsible idealists have compulsively competitive natures that seek fulfilment in the impersonal arena of work. It is there that they pursue their unsatisfied cravings for public recognition, personal acceptance, and power.

Work becomes the adrenalin-pumping "fix" that frees these perfectionists from experiencing repressed emotional pain from years past, unfinished business from childhood that lies buried just below consciousness. Yesterday's goals must always be exceeded because staying at the same level of accomplishment in their eyes is a failure. Pressure builds. Soon these driven individuals cannot *not* work without becoming highly anxious.

Overworking drains all their psychic energy as they make frantic efforts to control all the variables in a situation, and that includes people. They scarcely tolerate anyone who makes "unnecessary" demands on their precious time and energy, unless that person is *useful* in some way.

Because accomplishment was expected of them in their early years, ambitious and intelligent workaholics rarely experience anything but success. When setbacks do occur, or they fail at something important to their career, their shame and humiliation can be devastating. It was just not supposed to happen! No one must know! They will do almost anything to cover up their failures or misdeeds, even if it means losing their integrity.

When too many things go wrong and their defences break down, their repressed self-doubt and gut-wrenching fears roar to the surface. At such times, if others dare to challenge their expertise or threaten to derail a project, workaholics may erupt in rage and lash out mercilessly. Or they might retreat into a protective shell of secrecy and denial. Some stubbornly just try harder and senselessly repeat old patterns that no longer work.

As their feelings grow increasingly numb and flat, their self-serving narcissistic traits become more pronounced. Compassion disappears. As a consequence, values shift and an extreme pragmatism takes hold.

When someone is caught up in a "gerbil wheel" existence, everything else becomes a foggy blur. As one recovering workaholic put it, "Work was a shield that allowed me to avoid looking in the mirror to see who I had become. Work was a sacrosanct excuse to use whenever I wanted to avoid dealing with my growing personal problems. I had no clue that I was causing serious damage to others, and the thought that I had lost my integrity never entered my mind."

Ultimately, this sacrificing of *personal* responsibility leads to the saddest loss of integrity. Emotionally crippled workaholics can no longer be there for the people who love them the most.

Surely no one really sets out to have this epigraph carved on his gravestone: "Work was everything. Relationships be damned!"

WHO ARE THESE TROUBLED PEOPLE?

It doesn't seem to matter whether the fixation with work takes place in the arena of sport, industry, politics, social sciences, education, philosophy, or in the spiritual realm. One doesn't even need to have a "job" per se to be a workaholic.

Innate personality traits determine who will become a Controller type of workaholic, and who will be more the Pleaser type. The way these two types of workaholics lose their integrity differs.

Controllers

Prestige, accomplishment, and peer recognition bring the power these highly ambitious, often charismatic leaders desire. Early on, these so-called "control freaks" command attention and obedience. They set their sights high and are willing to take both financial and personal risks to get what and whom they want. They are usually found in top management jobs, or they work independently.

The level of narcissism in Controllers is unusually high. These driven bosses need to be right, and they expect much from those in their sphere of control. Because narcissists tend to self-reference and take whatever they hear within a personal context, Controllers are easily offended. Their anger and rage lie just below the surface, ready to erupt whenever others dare to differ.

In their false logic, two people can't both be right. The twist that always makes the other party the problem is: "If you have a different point of view from me, then you must think I'm wrong!"

Because Controllers tend to see themselves as superior and specially set apart, they may exempt themselves from following established rules and codes of conduct. They work all the angles and then justify their particular way of doing business.

Corrupt Controllers yield to temptation and take unethical shortcuts. They readily tell others what they want to hear, and then do their own thing. They neglect to follow through on promises and commitments and lie about what they actually did or did not say. Dissociation allows them to deny reality by pretending that such-and-such didn't happen or that someone or something no longer matters or is worth thinking about.

Their strong defence mechanisms allow those folks to cheat and lie if necessary to get ahead, or to win a power struggle with a spouse who resents their focus on work.

It is the Controllers' intensity, single-minded determination, invasive control, and one-sided judgment that lead them astray. Their awesome lack of insight into how their actions affect others makes them dangerous.

Power is seductive, and absolute power eventually corrupts, but it also protects. Former WorldCom chief executive officer Bernard Ebbers is a case in point. In a *Globe and Mail* article entitled "Reports Reveal Tight Grip of Ebbers on WorldCom," Paul Waldie and Karen Howlett describe how company directors rewarded Ebbers's greed and made it easy for him to leave. The board apparently granted him $1.5-million a year for life and accepted a promissory note for company loans of $408 million.

Ebbers had created a culture of secrecy and blind obedience in which executives were encouraged to follow orders and hide information, or risk denigration in public. One senior executive e-mailed this message when another employee asked for an explanation of a large discrepancy: "Show those numbers to the damn auditors and I'll throw you out the f****g window."

Ebbers viewed the company's attempt to draft a corporate code of conduct as "a colossal waste of time." He used high salaries and bonuses to seduce his senior managers to collude in the massive accounting fraud, and had revenue figures doctored to fit targets. A group of directors even met with the president of the Bank of America to try to persuade him to ease off on their investigations because of Ebbers's crucial role in the company. "Ethics be damned" is the moral of this heinous tale.

A luncheon companion and I were talking about how much corruption was coming to light in the form of insider trading and fraud charges against well-known personalities. This man felt that Washington's Watergate scandal had somehow given ordinary people "permission" to abandon societal values and blithely "do their own thing."

There is a real and present danger that the loss of integrity will no longer be shunned but almost admired. Andy Borowitz, the author of *Who Moved My Soap: The CEO's Guide to Surviving in Prison*, ponders whether going to prison isn't a sign that one has arrived! Government prosecutors, according to Borowitz's logic, are interested only in the next headline-grabbing celebrity case – "so the very fact that you were arrested, handcuffed, and eventually convicted of a felony is the ultimate proof of just how big a fish you are. If you were found guilty of hundreds of felonies, as I was, that's even more prestigious."

His words are a good reminder of just how powerful an impact familiarity and constant exposure can have in dulling our outrage.

Pleasers

Like Controllers, Pleaser-type workaholics have a deep-seated insecurity beneath their arrogance. Both aspire to the trappings of power, but their motivations differ. Pleasers possess an unfulfilled longing to belong that drives them to be needed, admired, and liked by their peers. For Controllers, achievement, recognition, and status are more important.

Pleasers are often found in middle-management jobs where they dutifully serve the boss and are loyal and valued employees.

Where the ego boundaries of Pleasers stop and those of another begins is hopelessly blurred. These enablers neglect to ask themselves an important question, "Whose problem is this anyway?" Consequently, these well-intentioned "fixers," as I call them, take on the added responsibility of others' problems. They enjoy giving advice and offering unsolicited solutions – that is, until they themselves become overburdened and start to resent those who have grown dependent on them. The resentment builds up on both sides, because those who are "helped" cannot take full and honest credit for their own work.

Pleasers are often startled when I ask if they can see any arrogance in their offers of help and advice. One client's reply is telling: "Well, if I can't problem-solve for my staff, what will I do? People are lined up outside my office waiting their turn!"

These publicly compliant "Mr Nice Guys" or "Ms Nice Gals" avoid any confrontation that might risk disapproval or rejection. In fact, some Pleasers would willingly sell their souls for harmony rather than make waves. They refrain from saying *no* when it would be appropriate to do so, and they rarely vocalize their suppressed rage when Controller-type bosses use them to look good by demanding unreasonable amounts of their time and energy, and then take credit for the Pleasers' work.

The loss of integrity for Pleasers comes mainly through sins of omission and subtle sabotage. Passive-aggressive, they neglect to tell the truth. They procrastinate and waffle when issues are contentious and then blame others when things go badly. They tune out of conversations, fail to respond, and then accuse others of misunderstanding or misinterpreting them. Or they conveniently "forget" what they don't want to remember. (See chapter 1 for more examples of overt and covert dishonesty.)

As their feelings are mummified and no longer inform their judgment, their dependency on others becomes a growing problem. Their spouses are expected to be mind-readers who should know what they want and be willing to cater to their personal needs, interests, and work priorities. These *takers* are caught up in what is called the "Mother Complex" – the expectation that someone else should take care of them and make them happy.

The reciprocal give and take of real love becomes scarce, and family members receive only the dregs of their energy and attention. Wives frequently mention how hurtful it is to see their husband at the office party being perfectly charming, full of fun and chatter, while at home he sits glowering in stony silence.

When Pleasers are overwhelmed by anxiety and fatigue, stress-related illnesses and psychological disturbances such as depression, panic attacks, and claustrophobia signal their distress. Those no longer able to cope must take extended sick leave.

For both Controllers and Pleasers alike, their one-sided relationships eventually lead to family breakdown. Their relentless pursuit of power and their perfectionism, obsession, and narcissism have cost them dearly.

THE PREDICTABLE BREAKDOWN
SYNDROME

The course that workaholism follows is predictable yet personally tragic. A number of specific fears, guilt, chronic fatigue, and the loss of feelings eventually produce severe personality changes that damage loved ones and cause associates and the public much grief. Integrity is affected at all stages of the breakdown syndrome. Figure

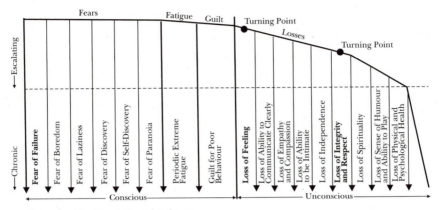

Figure 6.1 The Breakdown Syndrome

6.1 outlines the conscious and unconscious factors that cause workaholics to lose their integrity.

The Escalation of Fear

The values and behaviour of the workaholic begin to change when a number of repressed fears surface to consciousness and undermine confidence. These fears recede in good times, only to erupt with a vengeance when plans go awry. Weakened defence mechanisms can no longer protect the workaholic from a troubled reality.

"It's huge!" is how my clients describe their worst nightmare, the *fear of failure*. Whether the threat is real or perceived, it can set them morally and spiritually adrift.

To avoid humiliation, stressed-out workaholics willingly take questionable risks to shore up their endangered reputations or they use others to bolster sagging egos. When ethics or morality get in the way, they have no problem arguing that "the ends justify the means."

On the home front, they set themselves up for failure by denying their cruel insensitivity, lack of insight, and blatantly outrageous behaviour. Too self-absorbed, they hear only the criticism and fail to recognize the pain that others close to them are experiencing.

A *fear of laziness* drives their frenetic lifestyle. Workaholics want others to see them as hard workers, yet they tell me that deep down inside they suspect that if they let up, even for a short while, their laziness will take over.

Psychologically, it is true, these people are lazy. They seem to have little curiosity about what makes them tick or where their life is headed.

Here's how Margie, an office manager, responded to my challenge to take time out to reflect: "When you suggested I go down to the waterfront, sit on a bench and watch water for half an hour without moving, my stomach went into a knot. I did end up going, but because I get bored so quickly, I took some business magazines with me. Otherwise, people would wonder what in the heck I was doing just sitting there. I didn't want anyone to think that I was a mental case."

In this situation, the fear of what others would think prevented Margie from experiencing some of the positive sensations she needed to ground herself, to help fill up the emptiness deep inside. Sadly, she just didn't get the point of the exercise.

Her *fear of boredom* is real. When only the dark side of intuition works and the "big picture" is lost, workaholics do get bored quickly and become restless, impatient, and reckless. They want things *now*. Easily agitated, they make impulsive decisions that lead to careless mistakes and serious errors of judgment. Faster is not smarter, and efficiency suffers.

A *fear of discovery* heightens to panic as workaholics worry about the "visibility" of their mistakes. Secrecy and privacy become vital protectors. They can't concentrate, and their memory is like a sieve. No one must find out that it is taking them twelve hours to do what they used to do in eight. Trapped in the confusion of such internal chaos, they make up excuse after excuse and weave a tangled web of face-saving lies.

Crippled by anxiety, many sit immobilized at their desks, yet attempt to look busy because they must be seen to be productive. After one CEO was fired, the staff discovered piles of files underneath the sofa in his office. He just wasn't functioning.

The *fear of self-discovery* blocks insight. Workaholics use an external frame of reference to evaluate themselves, especially when they can no longer validate their own feelings. They must rely on second-guessing how other people perceive them. This becomes problematic when others who have been alienated by their controlling manipulations protest or challenge their slipping standards. Workaholics become highly defensive and reject any negative feedback that conflicts with their self-aggrandized image.

When their defences break down, and the self-loathing that underlies their cocky arrogance surfaces, hard-core workaholics avoid introspection at all costs. Opening up Pandora's Box is just too scary. The authentic whole Self remains an elusive mystery – but the persona they can do something about!

During our sessions together, those brave enough to confront their pain and isolation express their concerns: "If others really knew me, they wouldn't like me." "What do you mean, we're going to concentrate on my Shadow?" Or, "Promise me I won't hate myself at the end of this process!"

Paranoia, the *fear of being victimized*, traumatizes the workaholic as the breakdown progresses. Hypersensitivity, unwarranted suspicion, jealousy, and envy fuel their fearful outrage. Some withdraw into a protective shell, while others rule by threats and intimidation.

Controllers manage up well but manage down poorly. They weed out those whistle-blowers who challenge the wisdom of their choices. They establish a small circle of like-minded yeah-sayers, play favourites, and shut out everyone else. Ultimately, they trust no one.

Chronic Fatigue

As stress takes its toll, workaholics rely on their adrenalin fixes to keep going. Caffeine helps keep them awake. These are people who already talk fast, walk fast, and eat fast.

When the adrenalin system eventually crashes, they slip into a state of prolonged fatigue, like elastic that has lost its bounce. Exhaustion makes them irritably snappish and rude. They take dubious shortcuts and neglect to do what they should be doing. Everything becomes "just too much trouble."

Eventually their health breaks down. As Dr Archibald Hart warns in *The Hidden Link between Adrenalin and Stress*, stress causes the adrenal cortex to become enlarged, important lymph nodes to shrink, and the stomach and intestines to become irritated. There's an increase in the production of blood cholesterol but a decrease in the ability of the body to remove it. Capillaries and other blood vessels shut down the blood supply to the heart muscle, blood has a tendency to clot, and deposits of plaque build up on artery walls (21).

At this stage of the breakdown, physical and emotional exhaustion can be masked by hyperactivity or acute restlessness. Hyper types jump from one activity to the next, and often have trouble winding down at night. There is little awareness of how tired, cramped, or tense they are, and they even boast about not needing much sleep. Couch potatoes, in contrast, can fall asleep anywhere, anytime. They stare unseeing at the TV for hours, or escape to dens or bedrooms where no "performance" is expected of them.

Relaxation becomes impossible. A vacation can be traumatic, unless it is a brief weekend jaunt or a short holiday crammed with activities. Longer, more leisurely vacations induce unpleasant adrenal withdrawal symptoms that feed their compulsion to plug back into the office. Technology makes this escape far too easy. They find some excuse to phone in or insist on driving back to the city for some mythical "important meeting."

These bored but increasingly boring people make no time to contemplate where their life is headed. As J.B. Priestly put it: "Any fool can be fussy and rid himself of energy all over the place, but a man has to have *something* in him before he can settle down to do *nothing*."

This whole lifestyle raises the question of why workaholics, who claim to have integrity, would inflict a similar loss of health and balance on those they profess to love. Their "hurry sickness" is contagious. The so-called "hurried child" syndrome describes the situation where their children are driven from one lesson or activity to yet another throughout the week, and there's barely time left for purposeless, genuine play. No one gets listened to or asked questions when Mom is obviously exhausted but busy multi-tasking, and Dad is running out the door because he doesn't want to get caught in rush-hour traffic.

No wonder children are increasingly diagnosed with attention deficit disorder and chronic fatigue syndrome. The family's mantra has become, "Fast is good and more is always better."

I suspect that many cases of "yuppie flu" are indeed misdiagnosed workaholics.

Guilt

If our Feeling function is working, guilt acts as a healthy corrective response to irresponsible wrongdoing. It allows us to make an apology, ask for forgiveness, and make amends by changing our behaviour.

Many workaholics do make promises to work less. However, several months later, their spouses discover that they've been seduced into taking on yet another more visible and prestigious task.

As the breakdown progresses, however, shame, a combination of repressed guilt and self-anger, gradually replaces guilt. Directed outwards, shame transforms into ugly moods, put-downs, sarcasm, and rages. Inwardly directed, it punishes by inhibiting self-nurturing. Workaholics overwork, neglect to eat properly or get enough sleep, and then refuse to contact a physician when their bodies are screaming distress.

The Loss of Feeling

At this crucial watershed, the powerful Doing-Performing side of the personality has eclipsed the Feeling-Being side.

Edward, a recovering workaholic, has painful memories of what it is like not to feel:

> For me, not to feel is neither hot nor cold, but brittle and dry and eerily quiet. I can think, concentrate and calculate, and I do these things constantly, every waking moment. But though I observe everything, always measuring and evaluating, I understand little. I see every starkly etched detail, but the colours around me are faded.
>
> Everything is reduced to actions – questions and answers. And every question must be answered.
>
> Mystery and wonder are absent from this world of mine. Analysis has superseded them, and its companions, criticism and cynicism, occupy all the rooms inside me. Warmth and kindness are pushed aside, and there is a bitter taste in my mouth.
>
> My soul seems aimless and abandoned, with no lived past or hoped for future. This is emptiness, a life filled only with propositions, misconceptions and doubts, spoken and unspoken, all in ceaseless, compulsive succession.
>
> And yet, even in this agitated, murky driven state, I remember feelings. They are buried somewhere deep – ill-formed, inchoate, half forgotten. And I ache, and cry dry, uncomprehending tears.
>
> God help me never to live that way again.

Character Changes

Largely unconscious but profound personality changes accompany this loss of feeling. A series of losses diminish integrity as the powerful Dr Jekyll turns into an unacknowledged Mr Hyde.

Communication lacks clarity. Obsessive thinking becomes more inconsistent and circular, going nowhere. As thoughts are added or retracted, workaholics give out mixed messages that are too convoluted or cryptic to be understood.

Controlling workaholics want to make their point. It matters not that their delivery is short, blunt, and sharp, or that their messages are dictatorial, opinionated, and judgmental. It is the listeners' fault if they are left confused by bizarre twists of logic.

Such quasi-logical communication sounds like this: Peter, a respected physician, criticizes his wife endlessly but insists in all seriousness, "My wife and I are just fine. We're both intelligent, well adjusted, and mature. The problem is the relationship."

Outwardly, workaholics like Peter appear calm, controlled, and poker-faced. Inside, they're in a state of confused anxiety, yet remain puzzled about its source.

Empathy and compassion disappear. To be understanding and loving, one must feel and be able to express genuine emotional support and grateful appreciation.

Feeling language does this best. Maurice Boyd in *A Lover's Quarrel with the World* refers to William James's thought that by expressing an emotion, we strengthen it. Boyd adds, "When we express love we don't merely express how we already feel; we increase our capacity for loving" (90).

When love and compassion go missing, the Shadow side of the personality is given free reign.

Intimacy suffers when the workaholic is all persona and there is no strong sense of Self. During the breakdown, depression often inhibits libido and sexual desire. For many workaholics the sexual act becomes yet another "performance."

A strong fear of intimacy develops when ego boundaries are hopelessly blurred, and marriage vows to honour each other are thwarted by ongoing power struggles. In *Intimate Partners*, Maggie Scarf reminds us: "Intimacy is a merging and fusion of the self and other – which involves the threat of losing one's own separate personality" (362). Rather than give up control and risk self-annihilation, workaholics take an autonomous stance in the relationship.

Scarf describes the mutual frustration: "In truth, the intimacy seeker has promised to chase but never to overtake the partner, just as the autonomy seeker has promised to run but never to get too distant from her breathless, dissatisfied pursuer" (365).

No wonder couples remain locked in conflicts that destroy the trust, respect, and friendship necessary for real love. Many of the couples I see have not been sexual for years. There is no real intimacy in affairs because both parties can go home to their own world after. Distance creates its own barrier.

Independence turns to dependency. No one can claim to be independent if he doesn't know how he feels or she doesn't know what she wants. When Feeling information no longer informs judgment, workaholics struggle to translate thoughts into feelings and search for clues to know how to act or what to say.

Ask a workaholic how he feels, and he'll say what he thinks. Ask again, and the answer is defensive. Some fake a standard reaction by guessing at an appropriate response.

Roger's response is not untypical. When asked how he felt about an incident, Roger hesitates and then turns to his wife, looking for the right answer. He needs Connie to bail him out.

Yet five minutes later, Roger comes out with a cruel remark that just devastates Connie. He is acting out his own shame of dependency by punishing the partner he depends on. Connie has been trying to "help" her husband but is playing the role of enabler. Both end up resenting each other.

The *loss of integrity* takes place in incremental stages. Each time a person lies, cheats, or steals, it becomes easier, and the stakes inevitably rise accordingly.

At some point in the breakdown, the enormity of some wrongdoing hits home. A spouse leaves because of abuse or neglect, or a boss uncovers a fraudulent act. Whatever happens, the wrong is no longer a secret but public knowledge. The breakdown accelerates.

If shame and humiliation do break through to consciousness, memories flood up and workaholics experience overwhelming pain and remorse for their past actions. For the lucky ones, this is the turning point where transformation can begin. Unfortunately, those who can't face the reality of past misdeeds often sink into a state of deep depression. The fall from grace may be cushioned for those wealthy enough to afford a prominent lawyer, and those who do manage to avoid censure keep on telling the world they are innocent. Headlines scream from all the papers, and trials seem to go on forever.

For those who have *lost their spirituality*, or never had it, this is a grim picture indeed. It is hard to give up control and power if you have no faith or trust that you won't fall back into chaos. In their search for their authentic Self, many recovering workaholics rediscover their religious beliefs and faithfully attend their place of worship.

The *loss of a sense of humour and the ability to play* empties workaholics' lives of joy and laughter. They use a black, sarcastic type humour to defend themselves from getting too close or involved. They'll often respond with a diabolical laugh or chilling sneer.

These competitive people work at their play, analyse each shot, and drive themselves to win or score points higher than the last time. If things go badly, they use foul language and throw bats and racquets in frustration. Because they over-schedule, they often come rushing in to "play," frazzled and irritable. In the later stages, genuine play is almost non-existent.

The *loss of physical and psychological health* is inevitable. An early sign that the psyche has become rigid occurs when workaholics develop a stiff way of carrying themselves. Their movements appear robotic, and back problems are common. Their tightly crossed arms and legs, taut facial muscles, and locked jaws reflect their defensive attitude. But out of touch with feelings and body signals of distress, they remain unaware of the increases in adrenalin.

Those few who have remarkable stamina persevere at their work throughout their lifetime. Some never retire and work into their eighties. Privately they complain about aches and pains but stubbornly refuse to get medical attention. They can suffer from panic attacks, claustrophobia, chest pains and pressures, increased heart activity, abnormal blood pressure, stomach sensitivity and ulcers, weak spells, trembling and even paralysis.

Those who falsify reality can experience periodic retreats into a psychotic state where reality and fantasy blur. A complete disintegration of ego may occur, and suicide may be the tragic outcome.

As well, strokes and heart attacks often lead to sudden death. The Japanese have a word to describe death from overwork: *karoshi.*

THE SEDUCTION OF DENIAL, CONTROL, AND POWER

Denial plays a key role in all addictions.

When workaholics yield to temptation and their integrity is lost, denial becomes an essential ally in maintaining the illusion of respectability. Those who are past masters of "impression management" can sometimes salvage their tarnished reputations. However, well-defended workaholics are unlikely to have insight into what they have done to others.

In the following chapter, we learn more about the various forms of self-deception that people use to block painful realities. Awareness is necessary before workaholics can learn to transform denial into the truth that will set them free to deal in a healthier way with what *is*, not what they want things to be.

Control is a way to attain power, but it is also intrusive and offensive. Paradoxically, workaholics control other people with ease, but they themselves lack self-control and a healthy inner dialogue with their conscience.

"My mind's made up, don't confuse me with the facts," could be their mantra. Workaholics tell me that they *know* they're right, and their way is best. Control tactics make it possible to ram their ideas through. No time is taken to listen and consult or worry about whether others are on board.

With a cry of frustration, the staff of one recovering workaholic protested his scheduling yet another meeting. "Why did you bother? You had already decided what you were going to do!" This in fact was a good sign, reflecting on his changing attitude, as before no one dared to confront this dictatorial boss.

To give up micro-managing every detail to achieve perfection is no easy feat. Cassandra, once a highly successful entrepreneur who suffered a breakdown, recalls the tantrums she used to get into if she went to the store to buy apples but decided that they weren't any good. "I would scour the neighbourhood, driving from one store to the next till I found what I wanted. Now, I buy pears or bananas!"

A simple anecdote, but highly symbolic of the compulsive perfectionism that was her undoing. Happily, she adds, "I feel so much lighter. I'm not carrying the weight of the world any more."

Power can be used for good or evil, but excesses of power coupled with arrogance spell trouble. Advancement opportunity can be a seductive force that lures the workaholic away from the family.

I received a phone call from a woman in the United States whose husband had been appointed president of an international organization. Apparently he would now be splitting his time between home and New York. When she began to question his decision, his battle cry was: "Get yourself a good book and get out of the way!" When she protested, he icily replied, "You'll get used to it."

Telling me this, she laughed nervously, "Are we in trouble or what?"

Integrity flourishes only when the power of love wins out over the power of greed.

Greed arises out of the aggressive and acquisitive instincts that command a competitive edge. It is a world of lofty ambitions, strategies, tactics, manipulation, gamesmanship, and exploitation.

In contrast, power coupled with love and compassion has infinite possibilities for good. Its strength arises from the nurturing and sexual instincts that encourage empathy, compassion, sharing, generosity, good will, and compromise. Its language expresses appreciation and enthusiastic support for self and others.

Integrity is, after all, a moral choice.

The dynamics inherent in narcissism, obsession, and workaholism explain some of the reasons people lose their integrity.

We now consider the broader picture of how integrity's wholeness is threatened by the negative character traits that Carl Jung referred to as the Shadow side of our personality.

7

The Corruption of Character

Nobody can honestly think of himself as a strong character because, however successful he may be in overcoming them, he is necessarily aware of the doubts and temptations that accompany every important choice.

W.H. Auden

EVERYDAY TEMPTATIONS

The psychology of why certain people commit criminal acts is beyond the scope of this book. Instead, our focus is on resisting everyday temptations by affirming our admirable traits and becoming more conscious of our character flaws.

None of us can afford to remain naive when it comes to integrity. As Ernest Hemingway wrote in his posthumously published novel, *The Garden of Eden*, "all things truly wicked start from innocence."

AN INTRODUCTION TO THE SHADOW

Writers, philosophers, and scientists throughout the ages have tried to make sense out of how good can so easily be corrupted into evil. Albert Einstein described a poignant truth when he said, "The tragedy of life is what dies inside a man while he lives."

The choices we make are influenced by both the personal Shadow and what Carl Jung coined the "Collective Unconscious."

The Personal Shadow

Like the Roman god Janus, the personal Shadow has two opposite faces.

The *Negative Shadow*, according to Jungian terminology, contains split-off material we once held consciously but later disowned in order to evade punishment or emotional rejection. Our integrity is threatened whenever these blocked-off feelings and thoughts unwittingly sabotage our positive values and distort reality.

It is so easy to see other people's faults and to bury our own. However, we may glimpse our disowned foibles in projected form when we find ourselves overreacting to someone else's negative trait.

"Terry is such a liar," Violet announces self-righteously.

Suspecting that my client may be projecting, I suggest she try a reality-checking exercise I call "*bringing home your Shadow.*" I proceed by asking Violet, "Just how does dishonesty get played out in your own life?"

Using the examples she offers, we explore whether she has used an overt form of lying or the more covert, passive-aggressive style. This self-challenging exercise can provide useful feedback whenever we are trying to figure out why we've overreacted and done or said some irresponsible things.

The *Positive Shadow* contains the admirable but largely hidden strengths that remain underdeveloped, like muscles atrophied through lack of exercise. Strange as it may sound, we may not be conscious of our own integrity. We may admire a friend because of her refreshing honesty but fail to realize that we too possess this trait.

What stops people from recognizing their own self-worth? Consciousness may be stifled by a lack of will or curiosity. If we remain psychologically lazy, we will miss out on the fresh excitement of developing some unacknowledged talent.

Sometimes life experiences force character development. Jason, a painfully shy, introverted freshman, had always played it safe by remaining poised on the periphery of life, a passive watcher, not an instigator of change. His classmates in high school described him as "observant, yet distant and remote." Jason's capacity for empathetic generosity lay largely dormant.

By chance, Jason was paired up with an extroverted Political Science roommate who mercilessly egged him into joining forces on a summer tour of Europe and India. The two encountered some hair-raising episodes during their sojourn abroad, and Jason discovered that risk-taking can be both scary and stimulating.

His naivety crumbled when tricky urchin pickpockets on the Paris subway robbed him of all his cash. The two friends were struck dumb with fear after witnessing a Mafia-style slaying in Rome, and each was deeply troubled by the unjust caste system and abject poverty of India. These were not the same street people they had seen soliciting handouts at busy intersections in Toronto.

On his return, Jason seemed to blossom. His experiences revealed a social conscience that energized him to move away from his cautious stance to become deeply involved in campus politics. He joined several anti-poverty projects – as he put it, "to make a difference."

Integrity's compassion was now playing a key role in his emotional growth.

The Collective Unconscious Shadow

The *Positive Collective Unconscious* is the primordial wisdom that we carry deep within us. It is a powerful force that shapes our personal values and strongly influences our thoughts and actions. In essence, it consists of the information and knowledge each of us gleans from the many collective influences we experience day to day.

When we read stories and editorials in a newspaper, listen to commentaries on the radio, or watch a powerful television documentary, we are witnessing a range of collective values, some of which will influence us in profound ways. Through teachings and example, collective values are passed from one generation to another. Our family, the schools we attend, and the spiritual and business institutions we belong to all affect our views and values, sometimes on an unconscious level.

These collectives may influence whom we choose as friends or a partner, what career path we decide to follow, or which political party we vote for. We develop tolerance or prejudices that shape not only our character but also the environments we choose to live in. These selections may be the same or different from those our parents chose for us in childhood. If these collectives support healthy morality and strong ethical values, the Collective Unconscious can be a powerful source for good.

The Dark Collective Unconscious, in contrast, fosters destructive forces that pervade our lives more than we care to acknowledge. As the millennium advances, collective greed is frequently singled out as a major threat to world peace and stability. It is easy to condemn the Germans of the 1930s for remaining politically innocent about Hitler's intentions, says Eugene Pascal in *Jung to Live By*; if we are to escape collective psychic suicide and death as a nation, he warns, our own national Shadow must be confronted on a conscious level. Pascal's belief that ethnic and religious shadow projections appear to be growing fast in the multi-ethnic United States adds urgency to his warning: "Remember that whatever we misunderstand we tend to fear; what we fear, we easily hate; and what we hate becomes an incredibly magnetic hook for our wildest and most hideous shadow projections" (135).

In *The Art of the Impossible*, Victor Havel, the former president of what is now the Czech Republic, shared Pascal's pessimism. In his speeches and writings between 1990 and 1996, Havel described Central and Eastern Europe as a powder-keg of "growing nationalism, ethnic intolerance, and expressions of collective hatred" (62). History has already proved him right.

In "The Anatomy of Hate," an address written for the 1990 Oslo Conference, Havel explains that the totalitarian systems of Hitler and Stalin took a great toll on the collective subconscious. An appreciation of "otherness" was harshly suppressed by the tendency of such regimes to make everything uniform, highly controlled, the same.

Hatred, Havel says, has its roots in a desperate ambition, an unquenchable absolute longing to be recognized as worthy, powerful, or even superhuman, in possession of the truth. Those who hate feel they have suffered some injustice, injury, personal slight, or a questioning of their worth. Their hatred is targeted at a particular offender, or more dangerously, at some group that differs from them in race, country, ideology, religion, or social status.

Collective hatred, Havel adds, eliminates problems of loneliness, and eases the sense of powerlessness, of being ignored or abandoned. Hate groups attract morally weak, selfish, and intellectually lazy people who don't think independently. Their members confirm their identity through a sense of belonging, and aggressiveness is legitimized by the mob or pack mentality.

Racism's capacity to generalize makes it especially evil. "Otherness" is truly collective when people with different customs, traditions, faiths, or values are lumped together as targeted victims.

Fanaticism is the ultimate group evil, and members willingly sacrifice their lives to carry out the devious plots of their unscrupulous leaders. The world is still reeling from the terrorist acts of 11 September 2001 in New York and subsequent acts in Bali and London.

WHAT DOES THE LOSS OF INTEGRITY LOOK LIKE?

Only if we are consciously aware will we hear the Shadow's instinctive rumblings, its jarring vibes that warn of potential evil. Ernest Hemingway recognized evil, but did so only after the fact: "So far, about morals, I know only that what is moral is what you feel good after and what is immoral is what you feel bad after" (*Death in the Afternoon*).

Temptation often hits us at our lowest ebb, when life has thrown us a curve and we have hard lessons yet to learn. It bursts into our consciousness with angry rage or insidiously creeps into dreams and metaphors that haunt us. It pops up in a Freudian slip. It concerns itself with everyday stuff, not just the workings of a criminal mind, although it does that too.

Let's zero in on some infamous character traits that threaten our integrity each and every day: arrogance and intolerance, shame and seduction, anger and resentment, greed and sloth. (Dishonesty and wilfulness get special attention in the next chapter.) Note that all these negative traits relate to the seven deadly sins of pride, covetousness, lust, anger, gluttony, envy, and sloth.

Arrogance and Intolerance

Arrogance is a genuine or assumed feeling of superiority that reveals itself in an overbearing manner or attitude. It exaggerates its own importance by making excessive claims of position or power.

The false pride of arrogance breeds an intolerant attitude that someone or something perceived as different is somehow inferior. This disdainful sense of superiority can lead to acts of ridicule, rejection, exclusion, or scapegoating, all of which fail to honour another's humanity, worth, and dignity.

Before ruling out arrogance as one of your own Shadow traits, listen to Peggy's awakening tale. Sitting in my office, this clearly agitated executive secretary pours out a torrent of scathing opinions about the behaviour of her "ridiculous" father.

Uncomfortable about listening to this harangue, I stop Peggy and ask her to be more specific: "Exactly what does this man do that is so ridiculous?"

Peggy replies: "Well, when we line up for a show, by the time the family gets into the theatre, Dad knows everybody in the line! He's always embarrassing us."

"Do you mean your father is friendly?" I ask. As an afterthought, I add a further query. "By the way, do you think your mother is an extrovert or introvert? And how about your sister?"

Peggy admits with no hesitation that both are introverts like her, but she has never thought about what her dad might be!

"Your poor father," I respond. "He sounds like an extrovert, and you're berating him for one of his finest attributes."

Then I add my own sudden insight. "No wonder you're having so much trouble developing your own extroversion. It sounds as though you don't really respect it and therefore can't trust it!"

This confrontation was a wake-up call for Peggy, who needed to grow towards the more generous nature that extroverts naturally possess. She decided to make a purposeful effort to be more open and gregarious.

The couple moved four months later, into a new community, and the last time we spoke, Peggy was bursting with enthusiasm. She was telling me about the coffee parties she had initiated for her neighbours, and mentioned that she and her husband were already getting involved in community projects rather than keeping to themselves as before.

Peggy's concluding comment was, "I'm really enjoying our new home! And, by the way, I have a new respect for my father."

Peggy's story suggests a subtle form of bias of which many of us are guilty. While it may seem innocent enough on the surface, this false superiority stems from the egocentric, childlike "mine is better than yours" mentality – the narcissistic view that others should be like *me*, should want what *I* want.

Integrity treasures the concept of equality, not this up-down, winner-loser play for supremacy.

> Intolerance is the inability to tolerate difference of opinion or feeling or to grant equal social, political, professional, or religious rights to other racial groups.

Whenever we choose to be tolerant or intolerant, we are making a moral judgment.

Where arrogance breeds toxic disdain, personal intolerance raises our capacity for hatred. It causes us to criticize, disapprove of, and feel superior to someone or something else.

Intolerance manifests itself when we form prejudices about complete strangers. We turn into bigots when we refuse to acknowledge others' rights to hold differing beliefs or opinions. Equality becomes an inconceivable concept when we feel threatened by unknown customs or traditions related to race, skin colour, or sexual orientation. Even politics and social standing can set people apart.

Tolerance acknowledges such differences but chooses to welcome freedom of speech and diversity of thought and conduct. It makes us more open-minded in our attitudes towards beliefs that challenge or conflict with our own established views.

In today's permissive society, there's a fine line between what people consider moral and what gets labelled as deviant. It is therefore important to distinguish between taking the high moral ground by choosing to be tolerant and passively tolerating people or groups. Passive tolerance usually disintegrates into indifference, a more subtle form of intolerance. Charles P. Curtis points this out in his *A Commonplace Book*: "There are only two ways to be quite unprejudiced and impartial. One is to be completely ignorant. The other is to be completely indifferent. Bias and prejudice are attitudes to be kept in hand, not attitudes to be avoided." In short, the first step in confronting indifference or apathy is to acknowledge its presence.

Friedrich Nietzsche in *Beyond Good and Evil* recognizes the ambivalence inherent in this struggle: "Is living not valuating, preferring, being unjust, being limited, wanting to be different?" (39). Life for Nietzsche was about living to choose; his lesson was that we should profit from *all* of life's experiences, both good and bad.

To choose tolerance is to refrain from narrowly judging others and instead to attempt to take the understanding path, a journey addressed in chapter 10.

Shame and Seduction

Shame, a largely unconscious phenomenon, concerns the loss of pride, dignity, and honour by an individual or a group.

People can disgrace themselves by the impropriety of their behaviour or be victims of excessive ridicule, unfair practices, and emotional or physical abuse – any action that seriously negates their feelings of self-worth. At the time of shaming, they suffer acutely painful feelings of anger, rejection, or abandonment, yet later they may completely block out these bad memories. The resultant self-loathing, however, remains vaguely present.

Shame brings defence mechanisms into play that people use as protection against the unsettling fear that others will continue to judge them as inferior, stupid, or even idiotic.

As we noted earlier, shame avoidance drives narcissists to deny any evidence that would contradict their aggrandized view of themselves as good corporate citizens. "Looking good" in public overrides any real concerns they may have about actual personal or professional integrity. Ironically, their unrealistic blind ambitions leave them wide open to the temptations of corruption and seduction. Since their feelings don't register, they have little insight or concern about the impact that their manipulative dealings and grandiose schemes may have on the lives of others.

One way that people repress shame is to shift the blame for their wrongdoings and pay scant attention when others attempt to protest and challenge their reality.

Foster, a civil engineer, slapped his wife across the face during a heated argument around choosing a movie. He had never used physical violence towards Ellie before, and she was devastated. Lately Ellie had been attempting to be more assertive about her own rights and had been complaining to Foster about his lack of consideration for her needs and wishes.

"I treat all women with kid gloves," Foster said when I asked him for an explanation. As far as he could recall, the incident never happened. He "forgot" his abusive action – just as he had repressed his own father's abuse.

The circle continues as shame leads neurotic people like Foster to mindlessly punish others who thwart their wishes. The more frequent Foster's wrongful acts become, the more his self-disgust will threaten to break through his thick layer of denial. This unacknowledged shame increases the chance that he will consciously or unconsciously punish himself through neglecting his health. Foster already smoked and drank too much, and now he was working excessive overtime to avoid the tension on the home front. He put

off annual medical check-ups because he didn't like the doctor's probing questions.

Hidden shame typically has a way of coming to light in the next generation. When exploring a client's family history, I sometimes find that repressed shame is being acted out by innocent offspring. This unconscious phenomenon occurs when children are fated to act out some "family secret."

Virginia, a sophisticated-looking sixteen-year-old student, had recently become promiscuous, and together we were exploring why this was happening. She recalled a period of awful tension between her parents about the time she was ten. Her mother was often in tears, yet no one spoke about problems in the household. Eventually Virginia "forgot" and assumed that nothing was seriously wrong.

As we talk, she grows increasingly distressed and suddenly bursts into tears. "What's wrong?" I ask.

She blurts out, "I've just remembered something! Just as we were talking now, I suddenly felt a sick feeling in my gut. I've never told anybody about this."

She continues. "One day around the time I was telling you about, my girlfriend and I were walking down a street in Yorkville when we passed an outdoor cafe. To my horror, there was my father with his arm around a young blond woman. They were gazing deeply into each other's eyes, totally oblivious to the other diners."

Virginia apparently had hurried past so as not to be seen, and tried not to think any more about it. She was to find out much later that this woman was her father's secretary at the time, although Virginia had never met her.

Virginia's young mind couldn't wrap itself around the implications of what she had seen – that is, until she revisited this tense period. After the session she questioned her mother about what had been going on between her parents at that time. She learned that the affair with the secretary had been the first of a series of affairs that Virginia's neurosurgeon father kept secret from his wife. He had physically left the family to live with his head operating nurse when Virginia was fourteen.

Virginia was now unconsciously acting out her father's promiscuous habits. It was as though he had given her "permission" to be wayward.

Shame similarly affected Jeremy. His father, a well-respected lawyer, was imprisoned on embezzlement charges when Jeremy was thirteen. From that day forward, Jeremy decided that no one was going to have control over his life. Shame wasn't going to be part of his experience.

Jeremy left childhood behind and became overly responsible. Winning success and prestige in the community became a badge of honour, an obsession in the making. Unconsciously Jeremy was overcompensating for his father's disgrace by seeking public recognition and respect. He completely immersed himself in local politics and rose rapidly through the ranks. But an aching insecurity led him to seek glowing affirmation from others. He compromised his own honour by participating in questionable deals that bought him votes and the accolades he craved.

The sins of a parent have a powerful influence on innocent young minds. Whether it is a parent's sexual acting out or fraudulent practices, the child can unknowingly be at risk, particularly at certain vulnerable stages in life. The suicide of a parent, of course, is the ultimate shame. Unfortunately, that tragedy too is often repeated in the next generation.

Shame is really guilt gone underground. There the bad feelings no longer trouble the conscience and no correction is possible. Instead, integrity continues to be undermined by unresolved resentments that turn into an anxious depression that destroys inner peace by day and unsettles any hope for tranquil sleep.

The good news is that guilt, once acknowledged, can be experienced and grieved. Insight then can open up possibilities for future redemptive acts and forgiveness.

> Seduction emanates from outside influences that charm or entice others into corrupt acts or persuades them with false offers or misleading promises.

Seducers *use* other people or situations to their own advantage. Such people can be utterly charming when they want to possess something or convince somebody. These supreme manipulators make false promises that prey on others' weaknesses and balk when their prey refuse to go along with their schemes. They excel at retaliatory games like getting even, seeking revenge, or coming out ahead.

A young lawyer came to my office expressing a wish to salvage his marriage after a sordid affair with a seductive junior clerk in his firm. Although Sebastian had ended the relationship and joined another partnership, the young woman's husband was still relentlessly stalking him months later.

Sebastian described how he had got caught up in the crazy-making swirl of seductive approaches, which were quickly followed by sudden withdrawals. "I became totally fascinated with this woman. I didn't seem to have a mind of my own, and I believed everything that she said, even that she was single."

Now this troubled man had come to his senses and was trying to make amends to his wife. He had reached the point where he took full responsibility for letting the affair begin in the first place – a good beginning to a long journey of reconciliation.

Not only can potential sexual partners be seductive – parents can also persuade, charm, and corrupt. The following tale concerns an indulgent parent who expected his child to be a reflection of his own idealism, yet lived a lie.

One of my clients sent me the book *Frankenstein* because she knew I was interested in the phenomena of a Dr Jekyll turning into a Mr Hyde.

Along with others before me, I questioned how a nineteen-year-old author could write so knowingly about such pure evil. My conclusion after reading the tale, with the introduction by Maurice Hindle, was that Mary Shelley was really writing a story about arrogance, shame, and seduction. Her writing was likely an unconscious reaction to the unspoken dark contradictions in her father's character.

William Godwin, a philosophical radical of the anarchist left, spoke public platitudes of goodness and idealistic thought. His declaration that "Real knowledge is benevolent, not cruel and retaliatory" is but one example. Mary's mother, Mary Wollstonecraft, died of puerperal fever ten days after giving birth to her daughter, and Godwin's new wife was apparently not a caring mother-substitute.

Hindle points out that Mary was made aware early that she was the "unique progeny of extraordinarily gifted and famous parents." She also admitted to an excessively romantic attachment throughout her life to her emotionally distant father. This adoration existed despite her "decidedly reserved views on revolutionary, even 'liberal,' politics" (xi). In turn, William Godwin had high expectations of his daughter and deemed her to be something great and good – a seductive projection, to say the least.

This mutual idealized identification, often referred to as the "pedestal child" syndrome, occurs when a child identifies strongly with the opposite-sex parent and *unconsciously* acts out that parent's expectations, or alternately, guilt-laden projections.

Mary seemingly understood her father's arrogance and duplicity well enough to incorporate these traits into her main character, Dr Frankenstein. As Hindle points out, Frankenstein's gross error was "to decide with idealistic pride that *he alone* can put the world to rights through scientific experiment and the pursuit of knowledge" (xxix).

It is not surprising that the corruption of that idealism is at the crux of this tale. Further, we can only guess at how Mary's infatuation with her father and their mutual idealization played havoc in her tumultuous marriage to the poet Percy Shelley. A young girl would likely be seduced by the "coincidence" that both men in her life possessed a mad enthusiasm for science and a passion for reforming the world.

Percy Shelley was said to lead a double existence and during their eight-year partnership was often away from home. Yet he still managed to take partial ownership of Mary's success by referring to her book as the "fruits of my absence." Narcissistic people tend to see family members as extensions of themselves, so they have little problem taking credit for a spouse or child's accomplishments.

This hopelessly tangled web of projected seductions left young Mary with a gloomy fascination with the evils of duplicity, something her husband and father dared not confess. Whether the similarity between her fictional character and the dynamics in her own family was conscious, we do not know.

Anger and Resentment

Anger is an intense emotional reaction of displeasure, antagonism, or moral indignation brought on by a perceived threat of aggression, which undermines self-control or security.

Whether anger is triggered by shameful cruelty, censure, rejection, or abandonment, it is fully guaranteed to pull up the dark Shadow traits of sorrow, frustration, hostile fury, violent rage, and vindictive revenge. Since fear typically underlies the response of anger, self-protection, not integrity, becomes the focus.

On the collective level, all social movements arise from the righteous indignation that people justly feel when their public rights and personal liberties are overridden by the false promises of demagogues or dictators or the self-serving ideologies of corrupt governments. The moral outrage eventually sparks a rallying cry of protest that has echoed down through the ages: "We're not going to take it any more!"

At the personal level, taking ownership of our anger is paramount if we're to remain safe from its destructive powers. It is so easy to let loose whenever undue stress fuels our anxiety. All sorts of things start to grate on our nerves; a chance remark, someone telling us what to do, a rule we don't agree with, somebody not meeting our expectations – any number of triggers can set off smouldering rage.

Whether people are earth-bound or in flight doesn't seem to matter. Anger in the form of air rage is a modern-day phenomenon in which rage can be a Mount Vesuvius of pent-up frustration. Margot Gibb-Clark's *Globe and Mail* article "Attendants Fly Unfriendly Skies" reports on increasingly frequent incidents of physical assaults on flight attendants by unruly passengers. In some cases, people drank to excess after sneaking drinks from their own liquor bottles, and lost their inhibitions. Smokers also became distraught when smoking bans were strictly enforced.

Denise Hill, representing the Canadian Union of Public Employers, attributes this air rage to stress on the ground: "If you are under stress at work and all of a sudden you get on this metal tube and you're at 30,000 feet, you can't relieve it, so you take it out on people around you."

Resentment is stored-up anger resulting from a perceived emotional or physical injury, wrong, or insult that simmers or festers over time.

Social comparisons can be early sources of resentment. As children, we learn to evaluate ourselves through measuring our own and others' accomplishments or progress with some mythical yardstick. If we come up short on a regular basis, our jealousy and envy can quickly grow into hostile resentment. If these discouragements lead to a loss of spirit, we develop a "loser" mentality. Some children decide to disengage, to opt out of the race, concluding that "life just doesn't seem fair."

It is important to recognize that children fear something or someone long before that fear turns to hatred. The stockpiling of resentment takes place only after prolonged exposure to threatening situations. Such stored-up grievances can profoundly warp values into adulthood. These people have learned to expect little, and consequently figure there's not much to lose if they lie, cheat, or play the system to get ahead. Their anger and resentment typically feed into what can be referred to as a "tit-for-tat" mentality where revenge is sought to bring things back into balance again.

Bonnie, a social worker, was assaulted and robbed by an armed man who was railing against an unjust society. Sydney, a construction worker, had been abandoned by his father shortly after birth; his traumatized mother suffered emotional problems. Sydney had been struggling along at a poorly paid job, but after his company went bankrupt, he couldn't get work. He had a wife and three small children to support.

Bonnie had built up a huge resentment against Sydney after the attack and expected to feel vindicated when this thug was sentenced to a jail term. She hoped his imprisonment would help make up for the added trauma of the public trial hearings. "The funny thing was that the day the verdict came down, I felt empty and drained," she says.

Justice had been done all right, but peace continued to elude Bonnie. She found herself alternating between feelings of relief that this man was no longer on the streets and a confused mix of emotions that haunted her ever since that sentencing day. Sydney's wife had looked thin as a rail and shabbily dressed. She had sat through the trial completely motionless, and when the judge read the sentence, she slumped and slipped to the ground in a dead faint.

Each time something triggered Bonnie's memory of the assault, traces of her outrage were reactivated. But she was wise enough to know that unless she was able to go through the process of trying to forgive Sydney, she was likely to become another bitter and resentful person – someone capable herself of lashing out and punishing innocent others. She didn't want the cycle to continue.

Resentment is an omnipresent threat to integrity. None of us is immune from becoming the victim of assault, whether it is from an incident of road rage or some crime of passion or revenge – it's a scary world out there! Fortunately, sensitive victims like Bonnie are eventually able to let go of their resentments when their compassion wins out over the wish to get even. Alexander Pope put it well in his famous saying: "To err is human, to forgive divine."

However, forgiveness, it is wise to remember, is rarely a one-time thing!

Greed

Greed is an all-consuming and usually reprehensible acquisitive desire for wealth or gain

Greed, in short, causes big trouble. Its source is envy and a jealous desire to have what is admired. It fuels a restless longing to covet what others possess, be it money, power, fame, or lifestyle. Competitive types are not content with matching but must instead surpass. Their greed can inspire a voracious appetite for gambling, possessions, food, or drink.

There's no lack of ingenuity in the schemes of extraordinarily wealthy con artists who milk millions more dollars from an unsuspecting public. They're a dime a dozen these days! Once hooked on greed, individuals often become gullible targets themselves.

Ironically, greed is often used as a motivator in fighting crime. In fact the *Globe and Mail* used the headline "Greed was the bait for FBI stock sting" on an article by writer John Saunders. The US agency, together with the Canadian RCMP, set up a sting called Operation Bermuda Short to encourage money laundering. Apparently their scheme was a runaway hit, drawing people from "far beyond the circles first aimed at." One special agent reported, "We started to realize that people were lining up, literally bringing friends and family to get in on this deal."

In what might be described as an attempt to justify the integrity of the scheme, the superintendent in charge insisted that those caught had been told that cocaine money was being used, and so "no one was persuaded to do anything out of character." Participants had to be seen to be acting on their own volition and free will; otherwise the authorities could be accused of an entrapment scenario. The superintendent also assured the public that investors would not be further hurt by their operations.

A coveted object can also become a seductive agent. Many collectors spend far beyond their means because they feel a compulsion to add to or complete a collection.

A craving for glass art had taken hold of Trina, a young business consultant who could ill afford this passion. She often travelled to distant auctions that required overnight accommodations.

"It wouldn't be so bad if I could just admire the beauty of this art," she sighs. "But every time I find a piece of Tiffany glass, I just *have* to have it. Things have gone way beyond my control. Last week my husband insisted I give him my Visa card. What Charlie doesn't know yet is that I've also spent the better part of my aunt's inheritance behind his back. All that stuff's hidden in the crawl space in the basement – I don't dare display the real prizes! It's all too ironic, isn't it?"

Ironic, and sad – her integrity has been all but forgotten.

Sloth

Sloth is a disinclination to action or labour.

Laziness, apathy, and carelessness signal the slippery slide of sloth. Did you ever fail to speak up when some untruth was said about a classmate? How often have you stood by watching as a child was abused by a parent in a supermarket?

Did you neglect to speak out publicly when a co-worker was wrongly accused because you were afraid of losing your job? Do you take questionable shortcuts to save time? Slothful practices may begin innocently but are hard to stop once begun.

"Losing my integrity was like making a snowman," said Roger, an accountant charged with fraud, describing his fall from grace. "You start with an innocent enough mistake, and then instead of taking the time to search back through the records, you fudge it."

Roger's lost integrity had begun to roll down the proverbial hill. "Before I knew it, I was in big trouble. I never looked at where my sloppy bookkeeping was taking me – that is, until I started to get panic attacks in the middle of the night. When I did try to chase my mistakes, the snowball was bigger than me. By the time I hit bottom, it had run over quite a number of people!" Psychologically and spiritually, Roger woke up to find himself no longer in charge of his fate.

It's easy to fool ourselves into thinking that we are invincible, that it can't happen to us.

Sloth forfeits our freedom to choose. A wilful laziness can be soul-destroying. Any self-discipline we once possessed disappears whenever we choose to cover up a mistake, cheat on our bookkeeping, or neglect to return money when a clerk has given us too much change. Sadly, by careening off the path, we move out of a moral place.

Dishonesty and wilfulness play a special role in all our dealings from childhood on. Since honesty and self-control, the opposite traits of dishonesty and wilfulness, are crucial to integrity, they deserve special scrutiny.

8

Dishonesty and Wilfulness

Whatever is only almost true is quite false, and among the most dangerous of errors, because being so near the truth, it is the more likely to lead astray.

Henry Ward Beecher

DISHONESTY AND WILFUL BEHAVIOUR

Dishonesty stems from a hesitancy to recognize or a refusal to admit wrongdoing in order to escape punishment and rejection.

Whenever people want to avoid the suffering that guilt brings, they may find denial and distortion attractive alternatives to truth. This is especially true if they've found in the past that obeying rules, resisting temptation, or doing the honourable thing haven't paid off.

Let's look at some of the seductive guises of dishonesty: bending the rules, wilful behaviour, lying, and self-deception.

Bending the Rules

Dishonesty begins early, when children first decide to try out breaking rules. Testing limits within the family is a normal part of understanding the parameters of acceptable behaviour. By adolescence, peer pressure increases to either conform and adapt to society's rules or agree to participate in rebellious acts.

In the process of searching for the boundaries of independence, teenagers naturally rebel and challenge the fairness of their parents' admonitions. They chafe at imposed restrictions and moral dictates. They want to decide for themselves. By questioning the moral implications and consequences of following certain rules but not others, teens gradually develop their own code of conduct. Smoking, drinking, drugs, truancy, and promiscuity are popular testing grounds. Whenever illicit behaviours persist and become entrenched, moral development is delayed, and integrity takes a back seat to wilful desire.

Wilful Acts

Our doing the right thing evolves not from habit or instinct but from conscious effort and willpower. Doing the wrong thing happens when we abandon reason and compassion and do whatever we feel like to satisfy our current cravings or past unmet needs.

Defying a law for our personal convenience is but one example of a wilful act that ignores the common good. Do any of the following misdemeanours sound familiar?

Rule breakers run red lights, ignore stop signs, and weave dangerously in and out of freeway traffic. A sense of urgency sends adrenalin surging through their bodies, and subsequently ours. Speeding becomes a game, a strategy to get ahead. Other drivers focus on getting to the office by the shortest possible route and refuse to let other drivers into their lane of traffic, no matter what the circumstances. Pragmatism is their excuse.

Politeness is forgotten whenever people sneak into queues or push their way through a crowd. Manners are seen as a waste of precious time!

Words of apology are too rare when a self-absorbed parent keeps family members waiting or thoughtlessly cancels a "special" event. The children's hurt feelings or sense of abandonment fail to register. Irresponsibility is being modelled here, not willpower or duty.

The infidelities that often cause divorce and illegitimacy reflect the same self-centred, indulgent focus of those who choose to break their marriage vows. They are sacrificing personal commitment to immediate gratification.

Other-directed integrity, in contrast, is the antithesis of wilful self-interest.

Lying: The Deception of Others

Why do kids learn to lie? A toy is broken, a child denies crossing a forbidden road. A sibling screams in pain, and Johnny, who has just hit his sister, wonders if he can avoid getting spanked or sent to his room – a dreaded punishment for this extrovert. Introverts, by the way, often welcome such a reprieve.

Johnny is therefore tempted to blame his sister and yell, "It was Jennie did it, not me!" Instead, he decides to confess and say he's sorry. But he isn't at all, and he'll do it again when the circumstances are right and he's out of Mother's view. Johnny is not yet a moral being; he is doing the right thing, but for the wrong reasons.

Overworked parents who already have more than enough on their plate are loath to deal with petty nuisances. A childish tall tale is glossed over to eliminate any added stress, and so an opportunity to teach the importance of truth is lost. At the other end of the scale are perfectionist parents who are too quick to recognize deception in their children. A multitude of minute details consumes their attention as they obsessively home in and chastise the guilty party by lecturing and preaching, often going on at great length.

The irony is that sometimes parents overreact because they can see the child's duplicity – but not their own.

Children's reactions largely depend on how anger is handled at home. A child needs to be admonished for lying but encouraged to tell the truth without fear of reprisal. If parents are fair, they will admit it when they have blamed a child in error and apologize. They will be honest about their own shortcomings so that their children feel free to confess their own wrongdoings.

As adults, we must be able to differentiate truth from lies. William Christian in *George Grant: A Biography* refers to an address the Canadian philosopher gave on American policy in Vietnam at a Toronto demonstration in May 1966. Grant urged the students to continue their protests and bear witness: "We must keep alive in our society the recognition that there is a difference between truth and lies ... A society in which the difference between truth and lies disappears is a society doomed for debasement ... This is the one service the protest movement must perform in this society. It must break through the curtain of lies and half-truths and tell what is really happening in Vietnam" (260).

Clearly, in light of the shocking treatment of protesters at the Summit of the America's meetings in Seattle and Quebec City, our governments have not heeded Grant's warnings.

Neglecting to Tell the Truth

Too many people resist the notion that remaining silent, the passive form of lying, is wrong. It's much easier to rationalize "I don't want to hurt her feelings" than to figure out how best to diplomatically and compassionately present the truth.

A nonsensical statement such as "Finding out that she has terminal cancer will kill her!" has the intent of protecting a loved one from harsh reality. It also robs that chronically ill person of a chance to reach the peaceful stage of acceptance in the grieving process, before death comes.

We avoid responsibility when we only pretend we understand something. Hiliary, a successful business manager, shares her experience: "I let myself be ruled by fear because I refuse to let others know that I don't get it. Tuesday night, for example, I came into my office on my way home from a trip. In the middle of my desk, in plain view, I found a memo asking me to have some material ready for a meeting the next morning. The memo made no sense. Then I panicked." She spent a sleepless night as a result.

"At the meeting the next morning, I made up a whopper and pretended I didn't know about the memo." She sheepishly added, "But you'll get a kick out of this. No one else had the material ready either! The difference between us was that they frankly admitted that the memo made little sense to them."

Communication problems remain unresolved when people aren't forthright about what needs fixing.

Silence

Was silence a weapon in your home when you grew up? Did you witness your parents trying to resolve their different points of view, or were you forced to tolerate the awful tension created when two stubborn souls stopped talking to each other, sometimes for days?

Was one of your parents a moody, silent type who regularly exited from emotional issues? Was the angry spouse left as a result to deal with the emotional baggage of unresolved issues? As a consequence, it's not surprising to hear Jungian analyst Guy Corneau suggest that behind every bitchy woman is a passive-aggressive male.

In *Absent Fathers, Lost Sons: The Search for Masculine Identity*, Corneau describes his own experience: "My father's silence ... commanded me to remain always a little boy, in awe of his reserve – which I mistook for strength." He blames what he calls this "hereditary silence" for denying every teenage boy the need for recognition and confirmation. Corneau also felt that this silence lessened the chance that he would identify with his father as a means of establishing his own masculine identity.

Corneau sees the emotional pseudo-independence of men as a subtle form of self-absorption. He goes on to explain: "Men's dependence on the media, like a drug addiction, lets them avoid speaking, avoid inhabiting their bodies, avoid entering into relationships" (10).

Such emotional abandonment of others can be a denial of the authentic Self – always a sign of lost integrity.

Telling White Lies

No matter how well-meaning the intention, choosing to tell someone else a falsehood is wrong.

Lying is full of grey areas, of fantastical tales. When your parents were invited to a dinner party they didn't wish to attend, did you hear them utter some excuse that you later discovered wasn't true? You might remember being utterly baffled and even shocked when the guests who were said to be arriving the day of the party mysteriously never materialized. It was the first time you became aware that your parents weren't always truthful.

Rationalization is a highly developed art in families where parents distort reality to their own advantage. Children are left on their own to distinguish truth from a fabled reality, not an easy task for a developing mind when thinking is still concrete and abstract thinking has yet to be developed.

Breaking Promises

Broken promises are a form of dishonesty I find especially trying. There seems to be little integrity when someone you haven't seen for some time issues a vague invitation such as "It's been such fun bumping into you again. We must get together for lunch sometime soon. I'll give you a call!" You wait, and no call comes. You're disappointed because your eager anticipation has been crushed. You would have followed through on your promise to call and arranged a mutually agreeable time and place to meet.

This scenario is going to bother some personality types more than others. People who like closure and enjoy being organized have what is called a well-developed Judgment function. According to Isabel Briggs Myers, a researcher who based her work on Jung's theory of psychological type, Judgment-type people gather information and form opinions that agree or disagree with the facts, and then arrive at their own conclusion. Some make decisions with ease, others because they simply want closure. Both like finishing a process or completing an idea or task.

Because Judgment people enjoy scheduling and prefer organizing their lives well in advance, it is more natural for them to follow through with a fixed date for a promised get-together. They will also be more upset if someone else neglects to follow through with an expressed intention.

Perception-type folks, on the other hand, make series of decisions simply because closure is difficult for them. They keep changing their minds about what they want to do. Even when forced to make a final decision, they are still busy exploring other options before deciding to act, or are trying to find out what others are doing.

Because of their reluctance to finalize a decision, Perception types procrastinate, and getting together may be just one of the things they might decide to do. The intention to phone you up and set a date is forgotten as distracting alternatives rise in priority.

No wonder there are misunderstandings and resentment when these different types are involved in planning outings. Judgment people are likely left dismayed as to why that "irresponsible" person misled them by telling them an untruth.

This is but one reason why understanding and a tolerance for differences play such a major role in the development of integrity.

SELF-DECEPTION

Self-deception is the act or state of deceiving oneself. Deceit is especially dangerous when an agreement is presumed where none exists.

As children, we wish to be accepted and praised, so we quickly learn that it's smart to conform to the expectations of others by painting a rosy but distorted portrait of some wrongdoing. The option of protecting ourselves can be very attractive.

In normal development, the way we judge ourselves should progress from a need to be praiseworthy to becoming someone who is truly *deserving* of praise. As James Wilson in *The Moral Sense* cautions, the difference between pretending to be excellent, or really being so, eventually becomes crystal clear: "Up to a point we can fake honesty, courage, or generosity; but we know the difference between *really* being honest, brave, or generous and just going through the motions in order to impress other people ... We can fool our friends, but not ourselves" (33).

Unfortunately, deceiving others becomes a hard-to-break habit. Self-deception results when we fool ourselves as well. Clients often use terms like "phony," "not real," or even "not there at all" to describe how they felt before they began transforming their self-deceptive persona though an earnest search for authenticity.

Some people just never make that transition. A smart-aleck con artist vehemently denied that he had ever been a charlatan. His illogical defence went something like "Those poor suckers deserve to be taken because they were greedy! You want me to feel remorse for them? I'm doing them a favour!"

It's relatively easy to fool others, but in doing so, we must first fool ourselves. Writing about Helen Epstein's *Joe Papp: An American Life*, critic H.J. Kirchhoff notes that this influential producer-director began in the late 1930s to hide his Jewish background, "at first so he could get jobs, but later, apparently, out of habit. His second and third wives didn't know he was Jewish for years; his second wife, in fact, remembers that Papp used to ask her what Yiddish words meant – but then, he didn't tell her he had been married before, either." Now that's duplicity in the extreme!

Defences do have valid reasons for forming in the first place. This story reveals self-deception in action, but also the deep shame that Papp evidently felt about his Jewish background. His lies probably helped ease some awful pain, at least temporarily. The tragedy was that this brilliant man lost track of who he really was.

While self-delusion requires little discipline, self-confrontation takes great will power. And testing reality by seeking feedback from others can be just too scary.

Defence Mechanisms

Over time, our use of defence mechanisms such as rationalization, repression, dissociation, compartmentalization, projection of blame, depersonalization, and naivety will distort our own reality and that of others.

Rationalization

Rationalization is a reasoning process that offers plausible explanations to explain behaviour for which the real motives are different, unknown, or unconscious.

In *Everyday Ethics*, Joshua Halherstam writes that it was Plato who claimed that without rationalization, nobody could ever do anything he considered wrong. Plato believed it was an impossible contradiction to say, "I believe this is an immoral thing to do, but I will do it anyway."

Halberstam argues that we do commit acts against our better judgment. Like Greek philosophers before us, he says, we justify our weaknesses of will. "We backslide, we submit to temptation, and we excuse ourselves through a complex process of self-deception" (111).

Accountant Nick Hodson in his article "Lead Them Not into Temptation" states that people commit fraud when three conditions exist: opportunity, motivation, and rationalization. Opportunity opens up, he explains, when an employee has knowledge of a weakness in a company system or believes he or she won't be caught. A desperate need may also drive a trusted employee to commit fraud. The catalyst might be insolvency, the illness of a family member that requires costly drugs, or an obsessive craving for security.

When someone has strong rationalization capabilities, Hodson says, no such motivation is necessary. When people rationalize an action, "they are resolving a conflict they feel about that action in such a way that they can live with their choice and believe that they are an honest person."

Hodson quotes some common excuses: "Everybody's doing it"; "Business is business"; "I'll pay it back"; "They're not paying me enough"; "Nobody's going to get hurt"; "It's not for me, it's for my ..."

Repression

> Repression is an ego defence that banishes from our consciousness uncomfortable ideas, impulses, memories, or experiences deemed to be unacceptable or anxiety producing.

When repression is effective, we have no memory of some troubling emotional circumstance or past traumatic event. For example, Percy, a landscape gardener, told me that he couldn't remember any of his childhood before the age of ten when his mother suffered an aneurism right before his eyes and died shortly after.

"Could you describe your mom's personality?" I asked before this information came to light. Percy fumbled as he tried to formulate an answer, and looked embarrassed. In the end he had to confess that he just didn't know what she was like.

Percy hadn't been able to handle the pain of this sudden loss. Years later he was surprised to learn from a relative that he hadn't cried at his mother's funeral. Tragically, he had already become adept at repressing unwanted feelings to the point where *everything* seemed flatly vague to him. He described this state as confusion: "It's been like living in a deep freeze. I was distant, outside of myself, yet looking inwards on myself trying to discover who I really was." A little later in our session he said, "Nothing bothered me if I didn't want it to!"

Repression makes it easy to delude oneself into thinking that integrity doesn't matter. It also plays a major role in the dangerous defence mechanism called dissociation.

Dissociation

> Dissociation entails separating or disconnecting from consciousness any attitudes, impulses, traits, persons, or things that conflict with a desired positive self-image.

Through dissociation, troublesome people or things can "disappear" from our consciousness for a long or short period of time. In extreme forms, it allows us to believe that a person or situation no longer exists.

Temporary dissociation is not uncommon. Carmen, a harried young accountant, verbalized in our session her wish to reunite with her husband. Yet not five minutes before, she had confessed that while she was away on a recent business trip, she had spent no time at all thinking about the reasons for their marriage break-down. Apparently, she had barely thought of her husband at all!

When I confronted Carmen about the discrepancy between pro-fessing her intent to reconcile but doing nothing towards making it happen, she looked baffled. She then sputtered some contrived excuse for temporarily "forgetting" about Henry.

Dissociation is a powerful way to maintain a false reality. Its fre-quent use moves an individual towards psychosis, a state of no lon-ger knowing what is real. We need to live in a shared reality where we freely speak about our experiences and listen to the feedback of others. Sometimes our version of what happened will be affirmed and validated. On other occasions we may be challenged about our accuracy or the morality of our actions. Reality checks keep us on track. Reality testing is an important part of keeping integrity.

Compartmentalization

Compartmentalization involves psychic fragmentation, the isola-tion of separate parts of the personality normally held together.

Compartmentalizing requires that some fragment of the psyche remain separated from other conflicting evidence. For example, Gerrard, a medical practitioner, considers himself a generous per-son and a good husband. He focuses on his view of himself as an excellent provider. The fact that he hasn't taken his wife and chil-dren on anything but a business trip for their "vacation" doesn't count. He refuses to "let" his wife spend money on decorating the house or pay for lessons for the children, while he has a wardrobe of very expensive suits and belongs to an exclusive golf club where he lavishly entertains his cronies. All these incidents of stinginess with his family don't even enter the equation in his self-assessment.

Each negative facet of Gerrard's personality is like one of the boxcars on a long train. He focuses only on the engine out front – his proud label of being "the excellent provider." There is little accuracy in his limited view of his role as husband and father.

Integrity considers all the evidence in determining self-worth.

Projection of Blame

Projection of blame is a defensive technique that avoids personal responsibility by thoroughly disowning undesirable words, deeds, or traits and experiencing them as existing in someone else.

Projection is a blatant form of emotional abuse, the scapegoating of innocent victims by erroneously criticizing *their* mistakes and faults. It can be lethal to other people's emotional health.

The "Terrible Twist" is a term I coined to describe the unrelenting use of projection of blame by workaholics in the advanced stages of workaholism. These perfectionists, unable to love an imperfect Self, twist the truth around and hold others responsible for their own thoughtless acts or incompetence. They may use this cruel dynamic to punish a child, or a spouse, or a feisty co-worker who dares to challenge their insensitive words or cruel actions.

Rick, an estate-planning lawyer, arrives home three hours late for dinner with no warning call and no apology. Jacqueline, his frantic spouse, is in tears from worrying about whether her husband has been involved in an accident or, worse still, is lying dead in a ditch somewhere.

Rick hears only confrontation, not his wife's anxious concern: "Where have you been? Why didn't you call!"

He's not going to have anybody tell him what to do. Instead, he blames his wife for ruining the rest of the evening with all her fuss and bother. "I'm here now, aren't I? What more do you want from me?" Narcissistic people like Rick believe all they have to do is show up, and everyone should be happy.

To add insult to injury, Rick proceeds to attack Jacqueline's character. It is *she* who is controlling, selfish, and self-centred. He projects his own unwanted traits and sees them in his wife. His own thoughtless behaviour has been thoroughly disowned. The integrity he prides himself on at work is nowhere to be found on the home front.

When the Terrible Twist is used repeatedly on them, victims like Jacqueline start to question their own reality: "Surely I can't be responsible for everything bad that's happening between us!"

Reality-testing is hard when you're consistently bombarded with criticism over situations you didn't create in the first place. No wonder these abused spouses lose their self-esteem and become depressed or suffer from acute anxiety attacks. The worst part is that no one can predict when the next onslaught will occur. The person who is projecting blame may recover from a momentary psychotic outbreak of rage, but these frightening scenes are never forgotten by those who happen to be the helpless victims of this form of emotional abuse. There is no differentiation between truth and falsehood in projection but instead only ceaseless arguments about "who said or did what."

A phone call from a stranger tells it all. "Thank you for being born," says the unknown caller. "Without your explanation of the Terrible Twist, I would be incarcerated right now in some loony bin! It's taken me years, but now I know what's really going on at our house!"

For those who regularly make use of this defence mechanism to delude themselves and, in turn, warp their own and others' sense of identity, "integrity" is merely their own invention.

Depersonalization

Depersonalization is a non-specific feeling of the loss of personal identity, a sense that one is different or strange or unreal.

Derealization, the feeling that the environment is also strange or unreal, is part of the distortion of depersonalization. Today, many people feel disconnected from life-enhancing and meaningful human connections. The personalized contact that speaking directly to a real person satisfies does not happen with a machine message. Outsourcing of employees, home offices, faxes, and e-mails all contribute to this disconnect and subsequent feelings of alienation.

Heather Menzies in *No Time: Stress and the Crisis of Modern Life* describes a centralized "information-management system" devised by Accenture, whose parent company, Arthur Anderson, was implicated in the Enron accounting scandals: "Through it, the people seeking help from social services are standardized into computer-coded 'needs' and 'outcomes,' with set rules for working out the connections and quantifiable performance measures for tracking the results" (143). Individuality is lost as people become mere statistics to be measured, graded, or indexed.

This impersonal trend has serious implications for integrity. There is a lack of accountability when a person remains an Internet address, anonymously out of sight. Slavish followers who must conform to such predetermined systems or who get trapped in rigid cost/benefit analyses don't feel that they "belong." It is difficult for employees to be authentic when they aren't valued for their ingenuity or their unique contributions. Without personal freedom and the responsibility that accompanies authenticity, workers are set adrift and ill-equipped to determine or evaluate ethical guidelines. Powerless to determine policy and unable to grasp the larger missions and goals of the firm, these alienated workforces distance themselves. Loyalty slips away and resentment builds. It's little wonder that there is so much petty theft in the workplace.

Naivety: A Special Ignorance

Naivety is an ignorance brought on by a lack of experience, knowledge or perception of truth, rules, regulations, or laws.

Naivety is often a cause of lost integrity. Unaware and unsophisticated, naive people remain stuck in a childlike state of blind ignorance. They seem not only to lack general knowledge but also have little curiosity about whether certain of their actions might be amoral or unethical. It's as though a mental laziness is inhibiting their inner growth.

Such a lack of insight makes it difficult for them to differentiate right from wrong, unless harsh reality forces a correction. Some unintentionally do commit petty crimes, while other innocents become involved in more serious criminal acts.

Both readily feign ignorance when caught, and claim they didn't understand or know that some moral code or law existed. The truism that "Ignorance is no excuse" just doesn't register. It is sometimes difficult to determine whether the conscience of these naive Pollyannas failed to develop adequately, or their denial system works all too well.

Now that we have a better understanding of our own character flaws and those of others, it is time to offer some constructive ways to strengthen integrity. Expanding our self-knowledge by identifying our largely unconscious "Inferior function" is a good place to start. In Part 3, I use a self-awareness Gestalt technique to illustrate how we can improve our integrity by developing the positive side of this particularly troublesome function.

PART THREE

Keeping Integrity Healthy

9

Freeing Ourselves from Temptation

The strongest is never strong enough to be always master, unless he transforms strength into right, and obedience into duty.

Jean-Jacques Rousseau

Temptation and seduction are ever present, so our integrity can't be a fair-weather thing. When things are going well, we may accept the concept that half of life is positive and half is negative, but during difficult days it can be hard to see anything good.

Two thousand years ago the philosopher Seneca said much the same thing: "The trip doesn't exist that can set you beyond the reach of cravings, fits of temper, or fears. If it did, the human race would be off there in a body."

Integrity involves a slow transformation away from childhood's naivety and the relatively carefree and often careless days of adolescence towards the sober realization that if we wish to attain maturity, we must be *fully responsible for what we personally think, say, and do* in all circumstances.

One of my clients, Sarah, is telling me about her struggles around integrity. "I think integrity has got to be one of the trickiest values!" she utters in exasperation. This young mother is in the midst of a drawn-out court battle over custody. A year ago her husband announced he was leaving that weekend to move in with his secretary. Although Richard had spent little time with the children, he was fighting for sole custody.

Sarah describes her present state of anxiety. "It seems that every other day Richard threatens to do something nasty if I don't cooperate. Yesterday he was just plain vicious. It was all I could do not to lash back. I'm still so angry and hurt. Some of my thoughts really surprise me! How am I going to survive this messy litigation and keep my dignity intact? I do so want to be a good role model for my kids."

My reply went something like this: "The best way I know to resist temptation is to learn everything we can about the negative side of our Inferior function. By making our foibles conscious, we can begin the work of transformation by developing its positive attributes."

WHAT IS THE INFERIOR FUNCTION?

Many sceptics might challenge the disconcerting idea that we can help keep our integrity intact by becoming well acquainted with our Inferior function – the function most likely to sabotage our integrity.

There is great wisdom, however, in knowing how we typically behave when we're upset and more likely to lash out at others. Changing our reactions and staying in control then can be a real victory.

Sarah understood that her negative Thinking side roared to the surface any time she experienced rejection, her particular vulnerability. This insight allows her to go into a self-nurturing mode to keep her calm whenever Richard threatens her inner security. She now uses the independence and objectivity of positive Thinking to help her collect her thoughts *before* she speaks, so that the dignity she values so highly won't be compromised.

Let's look at how we can identify our own Inferior function.

In *Psychological Types*, Carl Jung succinctly describes the four primary functions: "Thinking should facilitate cognition and judgment, feeling should tell us how and to what extent a thing is important or unimportant to us, sensation should convey concrete reality to us through seeing, hearing, tasting, etc., and intuition should enable us to divine the hidden possibilities in the background, since these too belong to the complete picture of a given situation" (518).

Figure 9.1 is a schematic explanation of Jungian theory.

Jung believed that type differentiation is innate. People are born with one primary function that plays a dominant role in their personality. A secondary auxiliary function supports and strengthens

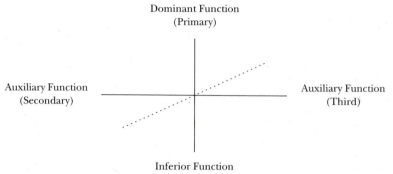

Figure 9.1 Schematic explanation of Jungian theory

this key function, while a third auxiliary usually plays a less significant role.

Jung called the least unconscious and undeveloped function, the polar opposite of the dominant function, the *Inferior* function. For example, if Thinking is our dominant function, the negative side of Feeling will be its Inferior. Or, if Intuition is primary, negative Sensation will play the Inferior role, especially when we are upset.

Let me explain the theory behind the diagonal line drawn across the diagram.

Jung believed that we should make a conscious effort to *purposefully* develop the positive attributes of our Inferior function, because therein lie many of our hidden strengths. By developing these attributes, we become better balanced and able to counteract our apathy, moods, depression, anxiety, claustrophobia, or obsessional behaviours – all warning signs of psychic distress.

Without self-awareness, we have little motivation to even recognize the need for growth. If we fail to "actualize" – to realize our potential through action – we may become dysfunctional and increasingly neurotic as all four functions shift towards their dark side.

For example, if our Inferior function is negative Feeling and something upsets us, it is likely that we will feel sorry for ourselves and become moody and sulk. Its victim-martyr mentality takes everything personally.

When the psyche is in turmoil, the body protests. Physical manifestations of stress show up as ulcers, heartburn, nervous tics, abnormal blood pressure, and a lack of vitality – the inability to relax or enjoy life. The body is screaming out that something has gone terribly wrong. The restoration of our inner balance is clearly in order.

WHICH IS YOUR INFERIOR FUNCTION?

Nervous laughter often accompanies the moment of recognition when I present my "What Is Your Inferior Function?" lists. This is a tool I've devised to help my clients understand the positive and negative properties of each basic function. If a partner is present, I often hear peals of hearty laughter. After all, it's relatively easy to see other people's flaws. The painful part comes when we must admit to our own frailties.

Many of us do readily recognize at least some of the attributes of our Inferior function, even without taking the Myers-Brigg Indicator Test to identify our personality type. This popular psychometric questionnaire, devised over fifty years ago by researchers Isabel Myers and her mother, Katharine Briggs, posits sixteen personality types. Our scores on this test, if it is answered with clarity, reveal whether we are Extroverted or Introverted, Intuitive or Sensation, Thinking or Feeling, Judging or Perceiving.

I suggest that my clients try to answer the test questions from the point of reference of what they were like as a child, especially if they feel uncertain about their choices. In other words, they are being asked: "What is most natural and therefore easiest for you?"

The lists in figure 2 may help those who are unfamiliar with the Myers-Brigg test to guess which of these four functions may be their personal nemesis. Also, it can be a useful tool when we are trying to transform our negative attributes into strengths.

EARLY RECOGNITION: PROPERTIES OF THE INFERIOR FUNCTION

The work of identification is made easier if we recognize that all Inferior functions possess the following six properties.

Negative

Some curmudgeons make negativity into an art form and manage to get away with it. However, a quick glance at the dark properties of each of the functions will make it abundantly clear that letting these trickers run the show is rarely wise. Playing these wild cards is like putting in a rookie for the last few minutes of a losing hockey game – sometimes we get lucky, but more often than not, we court disaster. Angry, resentful people alienate and offend others and often end up with few friends willing to offer solace. These judgmental people complain too much, blame others for their mistakes or unhappiness, and tend to use sarcasm and put-down humour.

Our significant others could tell us a lot about our negativity, if we chose to listen!

Primitive and Autonomous

The Inferior function is primitive, meaning it is not well formed and is poorly developed. It resists growing up and revels in the emotional roller-coaster that it creates.

In *Personality Traits: Jung's Model of Typology*, Daryl Sharp quotes from Jung: "The essence of the inferior function is autonomy: it is independent, it attacks, it fascinates and so spins us about that we are no longer masters of ourselves and others" (21).

This function is generally slow, yet strangely autonomous. Although largely repressed, it can suddenly be activated and produce disruptive emotions that result in atypical behaviour or bizarre fantasies. It spends too much time daydreaming.

Integrity requires us to be predictable and consistent in our behaviour, and this autonomous spirit works against that.

Childish

In an adult, while "childlike" may sometimes be good, "childish" is not. The Inferior function is like a wilful, petulant child who remains egocentric, self-serving, and narrowly one-dimensional. It acts out impulsively, without forethought or compassion. This spoiled brat does what it wants, when it wants to, without regard for others' feelings or well-being.

If we fail to develop our Inferior function, we will lose the precious qualities that encourage curiosity and adventuresome fun. Our imaginative drive to seek out interesting and exciting things to do or think about also will be limited. Intense people often lose

Figure 9.2 What Is Your Inferior Function?

SHADOW SIDE	HEALTHY SIDE
NEGATIVE THINKING	POSITIVE THINKING
Idealistic, perfectionistic	Realistic, principled
Irrational	Rational
Illogical, distort	Logical, analytical
Dependent on outside affirmation	Independent evaluation
Aloof	Involved
Subjective point of view	Objective viewpoint
Tangential, cryptic, confusing	Focused, precise, clear
Judgmental, high expectations	Fair assessment, reasonable
Sceptical	Open-minded
Arrogantly opinionated	Reasoned personal opinion
Erratic, unpredictable	Reliable, predictable
Overly competitive, aggressive	Competitive, assertive
Envious, jealous	Supportive, loyal
"Help" or "fix" others	Problem-solving skills
Controlling	In control
Overly responsible	Responsible
Obsessive, narrowly focused	Organize facts, ideas
Overly sensitive	Tough-minded
Uncomfortable dealing with feelings	Task-oriented, impersonal
Hurtful without knowing it	Businesslike, short
Reprimand, scold, lecture, preach	Explain own reasoning

SHADOW SIDE	HEALTHY SIDE
NEGATIVE FEELING	POSITIVE FEELING
Moody, repress feelings	Handle full range of feelings
Withdrawn, reserved, secretive	Sociable, friendly, open
Overly generous pleaser	Caring, concerned, respectful
Distant, discourteous	Warm, polite, courteous
Neglect to tell the truth	Honest
Personally irresponsible	Responsible, dependable
Takes everything personally	Sensitive
Inconsiderate	Considerate
Careless, indiscreet	Thoughtful, tactful
Self-doubting, insecure bravado	Self-assured, humble
Naive	Insightful
Overly focused on others, selfless	Self and Other-directed
Conditional expectations	Unconditional regard
Complaining	Supportive attitude
Intolerant	Accepting, tolerant
Self-sacrificing, martyr-victim	Firmly assertive
Quarrelsome, grouchy, unruly	Conciliatory, value harmony
Give in, defer	Consult, negotiate
Impatient	Patient
Easily discouraged	Committed, follow through
Mean-spirited, selfish	Generous, unselfish
Avoid unpleasant confrontation	Diplomatic and gracious
Neglect to compliment others	Praise and give affirmation

Dorothy was back being the compassionate Feeler she was meant
to be. Her goal had always been to be an understanding, non-
judgmental person.

Since this incident, Dorothy has worked extra hard on developing the objective, positive side of her Thinking. She counts to
ten before she acts to give her time to analyze why someone
might be saying something derogatory or acting out in a particular way.

Several weeks later, she came in clearly relieved. "I've actually
been managing to keep old Ethel at bay!" That's what she calls her
overly sensitive, "poor me" negative Feeling side. She now knows
that if she doesn't stay on the alert, "Ethel" automatically activates
"Fred" – her name for the "bitchy-witchy" negative Thinking side of
her personality.

I shared an insight with Dorothy that I'd gained from using Gestalt therapy techniques with other clients. I use the chairs in my
office to represent the different functions that make up the personality. When I'm asking my clients to explore their Thinking
and Feeling functions, I place four of these chairs as shown in figure.

I have discovered that intuitively I seemed to direct my clients
to a chair diametrically opposite to their Inferior function, the one
they were sitting in as they attempted to re-enact some acting-out or
"give-in" reaction, their response in a difficult situation. After
having them to sit in the opposite chair, I ask them to comment on
their negative behaviour.

After this exploration, I ask them to move to the chair that represents the positive side of their Inferior function. By exercising
this weaker function, they learn to give it a stronger voice in their
personality. Doing this Gestalt exercise, many clients discover
that the positive side of their Inferior function barely works. Sitting in that chair, they find themselves immobilized and almost
speechless.

When Dorothy was discussing the altercation with her boss, she
was sitting in the negative Thinking chair, which she calls Fred. I
asked her to move to the opposite positive Feeling chair so that she
could formulate some compassionate and self-nurturing questions
with which to confront her Inferior nemesis. After many false starts,
she began to ask "Fred" the questions shown on p. 153.

Figure 9.2 (continued)

SHADOW SIDE	HEALTHY SIDE
NEGATIVE INTUITION	**POSITIVE INTUITION**
Make errors of facts, not precise	Visionary, "big picture" focus
Faulty sixth sense	Unconscious gathering of data
Slow to figure things out	Answers "pop up" unexpectedly
Uncertain, puzzled, confused	Wise, "knows" what's right
Impulsive about reaching conclusions	Quick to conclusions
Distrust gut reaction	Trust gut reaction
Cleverness dulled	Ingenious, imaginative, clever
Head in the clouds, fantasize	Curious, original
Limited ideas	Brainstorm, generate new ideas
Creativity dulled	See endless possibilities
Fearful about future	Future-oriented
Resist change, new ideas	Enjoy solving new problems
Bored with repetition, routine	Enjoy complicated situations
Follow misguided inspirations	Creatively inspired
Mistakes in judgment	Good judge of people
Lose objectivity	Remain objective, stand back
Lose perspective	Keep things in perspective
Unclear about priorities	Know what is most important
Pessimistic	Optimistic
Threatened by too much detail	Like theory, abstract, symbolic
Impulsive, want it now	Delay gratification for future gain
Restless, impatient	Love life is as it could be
Neglects language, reading	Fascinated by language/books

SHADOW SIDE	HEALTHY SIDE
NEGATIVE SENSATION	**POSITIVE SENSATION**
Unrealistic	Realistic, see what is there
Short-sighted views	Observant
Dualistic thinking, limited options	Thorough gathering of data
Overly detailed, picky	Present detailed picture
Overly concrete	Concrete in perception
Flighty	Down-to-earth, grounded
Impractical, silly	Practical, sensible
Dwell on past regrets	Present and past-oriented focus
Discontent, dissatisfied	Fun-loving, content, satisfied
Get mired in details	Step-by-step learning
Dualistic black/white thinking	Consider all options
"Show me," "prove it"	Illustrate through examples
Selective scanning	Seek out all facts, figures
Selective listening	Use all five senses
Overwork a project, overcorrect	Thorough, efficient but slow
Distrust the process	Process-oriented
Rigidly follow rules, regulations	Respect rules, tradition
Distrust others' words/writings	Trust own experience
Resist learning new skills	Rely on tried-and-true skills
Wary of experimenting, new ways	Like established, proven ways
Rigid about routines, precision	Enjoy routine, being precise
Want what others have	Delight in possessions, beauty
Seek extra stimulation, highs	Value security, stability
Overspend, frivolous, greedy	Appreciative of simple things

their ability to truly play – that is, with no need to keep score or worry about who is winning. This is such a shame because childlike silliness and good-hearted humour are wonderful stress-relievers when adult responsibilities temporarily drag us down.

Stubborn and Rigid

Stubbornness and rigidity are both clear signs that the unconscious Inferior function is busily at work. Unacknowledged fears unwittingly cause us to dig in our heels or set down unreasonable limits. We stick to the tried and true, what is known and comfortable. We refuse to remain open or receptive when we fixate on some idea and insist on upholding it, no matter what evidence there is to the contrary.

Shyness is a form of passive stubbornness, a refusal to give of one-self. A reserved stance can be misinterpreted as judgmental or arrogant. Intense defiance or ungenerous acts serve to set us apart. As a result, many "shy" people remain isolated and lonely.

Rigidity eventually sets in when our stubbornness takes a firm hold. Our options subsequently continue to narrow.

Naive

Naivety is being "deficient in worldly wisdom or informed judgment," according to *Webster's Dictionary*.

If the Inferior function becomes disruptive and we act out frequently, our ability to concentrate and learn new information suffers. In contrast, a well-balanced individual usually has wide interests, reads mind-expanding articles or books, and does not shy away from controversial or provocative new thinking. When our life experience and knowledge are limited, our confidence and the capacity for discovering newfound wisdom are diminished and we remain one-sidedly naive.

It is my hope that the above descriptions help you to identify your own Inferior function. Next time you find yourself slipping into a mood, becoming stubborn, or acting childishly, pause and take a deep breath. Beware – you're probably under its negative spell!

It's never a good idea to have our Shadow working against us. Through heightened self-awareness, we can learn to protect ourselves and others from its aberrant behaviour.

USING SELF-AWARENESS TO IMPROVE INTEGRITY

Doubting Thomas types will resist the work of trans[...] protesting, "Why should I rock the boat? I'd just as s[...] all that dark stuff conscious, thank you very much![...] too much effort, and I'm already busy enough!"

If integrity is not clearly evident in our daily life, h[...] a sham. We all face ethical and moral tests in our [...] ings with others. How we choose to handle sma[...] likely be a good indicator of how we'll behave wh[...] issues challenge our resolve.

Dorothy, a medical researcher, describes how [...] lists to ensure that her integrity wins out in the [...] laughingly that she always carries her copy of the [...] she calls it, "in case of emergencies."

"The other day I completely lost my cool. I wa[...] thing that happened in the lab that I didn't ev[...] boss did one of his usual dumps and was blam[...] made in a measurement. That was the last str[...] the overtime I've done correcting his mistak[...]

Words just flew out of her mouth. "You i[...] up, you don't even know whether you're co[...] out of the room crying and found herself si[...] the Science building.

Dorothy continues: "That's when I ope[...] my lists. It didn't take me long to figure [...] had automatically set off my darned o[...] going to be the death of me yet!"

Dorothy was devastated by her boss's [...] they weren't true. Her overly sensitiv[...] hurtful – a "tit-for-tat" exchange. She [...] as good as she got. Yet on a consciou[...] aghast at watching such behaviour in [...]

Her integrity had suffered a blow [...] proceeded to make amends for he[...] would have been proud of me. I go[...] in, and apologized to that poor g[...] wife asked him to leave. He really [...] fool of him in front of the other t[...]

Figure 9.3 Exploring Thinking and Feeling functions

- How could you have expressed your angry feelings differently, without attacking your boss?
- Were you upset about anything else that day *before* that unfortunate exchange?
- What's going to happen to your self-esteem if you keep firing off like that?
- Can you afford to pump that excess adrenalin into your system when your blood pressure is already too high?

I then asked Dorothy to move to her *positive Thinking* chair. "Could you now think of some relevant 'lawyer-like' questions to ask Fred?" It's not surprising that this Feeler found these questions even more difficult. This is what she came up with:

- Do you think your response was fair?
- Is it smart to give your boss the power to hurt you with his blaming tactics?
- Do you think the boss's reprimand was directly connected to the overtime you spent correcting his mistakes?
- Do you have valid evidence that your boss's efficiency and accuracy has slipped because of his marital problems?

We can gain a more balanced perspective by learning to ask both Feeling and Thinking questions. No matter how trivial or serious the problem, information-gathering plays a key role in keeping our integrity.

Integrity can be so quickly compromised. Perhaps David's dilemma will clarify how this Gestalt exercise helped a Thinking-type person gain insight into the positive side of his Inferior Feeling.

David, a naturally strong, independent Thinker, exercises his analytical skills in his law practice with expertise. Because his Feeling function has been largely repressed, he hasn't recognized his own deep fear of intimacy. It makes sense that someone as independent as David might have problems letting go of his need to be in control. Authoritarian behaviour makes the sharing aspects of intimacy difficult indeed.

David's wife, Jill, was busy all Saturday running a fun fair in the neighbourhood with their two young children in tow. David missed her bubbly personality and found himself growing more and more amorous during the day. For people with intimacy problems, keeping distant from the partner or even just talking on the phone can be a real turn-on. After all, distance gives the illusion of relative safety.

It's not hard to imagine the following scenario. David was determined to get Jill into bed as soon as possible – linear thinking loves going from idea A to goal B.

The last thing on Jill's mind when she arrived home at 7.30 P.M. was sex. She was totally wiped out. Her refusal devastated David because, in typical fashion, he took Jill's rejection personally. He spent the rest of the weekend caught up in a foul mood. David spends a lot of time in the martyr-victim role.

In turn, Jill avoided David as best she could. As a Feeling-type person who values harmony at any cost, she wasn't about to sacrifice her well-being to her husband's bad mood.

When he again tried to initiate sex late on Sunday night and was rebuffed, he screamed at Jill, "You're frigid!" But Jill had no interest in being sexual with her husband when he hadn't spoken to her all weekend and glared at her any time their paths crossed. She also resented that David rarely took part in the children's activities. She had spent yet another day on Saturday being a "single" mother! Both went back to work on Monday feeling totally alienated from one another and depressed in general about their marriage.

Relating this tale in my office, David has some uncertain misgivings about blaming Jill for causing the messy scene that ensued. Projecting blame is the nasty side of his best function, his Thinking.

David is still deeply ensconced in his moodiness. I suggest he revisit the scene in order to better understand his reactions. I ask him to move diagonally to sit in the *Inferior Feeling* chair.

David sits slumped way down in the chair as he re-experiences his angst. He looks thoroughly defeated as he plays out the martyr- victim role to the hilt.

"What would *positive Thinking* ask you right now?" I query. David moves across to that chair.

I do some coaching. "Play the hard-nosed lawyer – keep objective and ask that sad guy over there some pertinent questions."

I warn David to take care in this intervention to abide by the rule that *positive functions only ask questions.* There is to be no "helping" or "fixing," no telling the other function what it should or shouldn't do.

My point here is to help David develop his understanding capabilities, to forego his tendency to judge and instruct. Thinkers have a hard time not problem-solving for others, so he looks surprised. But he proceeds to study the part of himself that he calls "The Wimp."

"Well," he says, "I guess that I might ask something like:"

- Did you really need to take Jill's decision not to be sexual as a personal affront?
- Does she turn you down very often?
- Do you think the way you handled this situation was fair to her?

This last question is an important one, because David values fairness highly. In fact, it guides his legal work.

David returns back to his "Wimp" chair and proceeds to answer. Thinking's objectivity and sense of fairness should help him consider the situation from Jill's perspective. He cannot see the whole picture when he is wallowing in self-pity.

The ultimate goal of this exercise is to help David develop the positive side of his *Inferior Feeling.* He needs its language and behaviour to be able to say loving things in addition to the thoughtful acts that he occasionally does perform. By growing psychologically, he is increasing his capacity for intimacy.

Later we discuss what David might do to correct this unhappy incident. First, he decides to apologize for his nasty verbal attack on Jill. He inflicted his angry mood onto her and neglected to tell her what had made him so grumpy.

David then tries to use his growing capacity for self-nurturing to handle his own mood and thus restore his equilibrium.

He does realize that it will take quite a while before Jill will be able to trust him again, but he has already begun acting on his promise to play a more active role in the children's lives by choosing to keep his weekends work free.

David then replays how he should have handled himself that day. "My first concern should have been to be there for Jill, not just expect her to be always there for me. I could have had dinner ready for my family and then drawn a bath for Jill to relax while I put the children to bed."

This Gestalt exercise helped David recognize his own self-centredness and his unhealthy habit of bottling up his anger. In his family of origin, if something went badly, it always paid off to stay quiet or leave the scene. He slowly begins to understand that this moody withdrawal sends signals of abandonment to Jill. She is left with no way of finding out why he is acting the way he is, short of having to drag it out of him. Early on in their relationship, Jill quickly tired of "fishing" for information whenever David clammed up. She has no interest in being his mother.

Next time you find yourself reacting to someone else's negative actions, try to use all your senses to focus in on your reaction. Pay attention to your body. Do you feel your stomach growing queasy, or are you clenching your jaw? Listen to your tone of voice. Can you hear its jarring pitch? Is your message sounding short, blunt, and sharp? Do you sound irritable and cranky? Are you lashing out and blaming others?

It's best not to ignore these early warning signs, because profound personality changes can take place whenever the dark Shadow traits take charge and sabotage growth.

DEVELOPING GOOD JUDGMENT

Good judgment comes when we use both our Thinking and Feeling functions to problem-solve. By developing the positive attributes of our Shadow traits, we begin a rich and fun adventure. It's like walking through a mysterious doorway and entering into a new country where everything is strange and unfamiliar, yet oddly fresh and exciting. By exploring new facets of our personality, we'll no longer be bored or boring.

In *Listening with the Third Ear*, Dr Theodor Reik, a student of Sigmund Freud, recalls meeting his professor on one of his daily walks. Reik sought advice about several personal matters.

In response, Freud spoke from his own experience: "When making a decision of minor importance, I have always found it advantageous to consider all the pros and cons. In vital matters, such as the choice of mate or a profession, the decision should come from the unconscious, from somewhere within ourselves ... we should be governed, I think, by the deep inner needs of our nature" (7).

The "third ear" is Reik's expression for tuning into the unconscious, to "catch what other people do not say, but only feel and think" (146). This intuitive sense hears the inner voices that would otherwise be drowned out by the chatter of our conscious thought-processes.

If we are to develop the wise judgment necessary to protect our integrity, a good "rule of thumb" is: *Let the positive side of all of your functions inform your decisions.* Keep open to new information, ask smart questions, listen carefully to intuitive rumblings, and use all your senses to fill in the details.

If integrity is to be a *proactive* choice, then the attitude we bring to a situation is important. We can choose to try to understand why other people do and say things, or we can decide to sit in judgment and critique each and every negative action. In other words, we can choose to be understanding or judgmental.

10

Integrity Is Our Choice

This act of choosing is the ultimate human act.
George Grant

THE ACT OF CHOOSING

In *George Grant: A Biography*, William Christian quotes from a letter that philosopher George Grant wrote to a colleague in support of academic freedom and the importance of choice: "Equality should be the central principle of society since all persons, whatever their condition, must freely choose to live by what is right or wrong. This act of choosing is the ultimate human act ... Our moral choices matter absolutely in the scheme of things" (213).

While morality and ethics are imposed externally through societal dictates, integrity stems from an *internal* state of being. The personal attitudes and values that we bring to decision-making are thus vitally important whenever issues of integrity are at stake.

Ultimately integrity survives best when our choices are *consciously* considered and not subject to our unrecognized greed, envy, jealousy, laziness, or obsessive desire.

Discerning integrity, I believe, requires a compassionate eye. Informed decisions based on hard facts and figures, or stringent rules and regulations, rarely represent the whole story. Our moral choices must also show a genuine concern for the welfare of others. This is not to downplay the role of thinking in formulating opinions, but wise moral choices are made when intelligence, compassion, and maturity come together to guide our judgments.

IS MY REACTION BASED ON UNDERSTANDING OR CRITICAL JUDGMENT?

Which path do we choose when a moral or ethical dilemma presents itself? The empathy and compassion needed for understanding are difficult attitudes to maintain at the best of times. Too quickly, we label others' actions as irresponsible or immoral.

The complex and onerous task of understanding why someone did something is captured beautifully in a client's apt metaphor: "Understanding, it seems to me, is a bit like peeling an onion. The more layers you peel off, the clearer and more translucent and delicate the next layer seems."

By taking the time to plumb the depth of our own compassionate nature, we capture the vulnerability of the human spirit.

Figure 10.1 is a guide that looks at the difference between understanding and judgmental values. Note that compassionate understanding stems from positive Feeling traits, while negative Thinking underlies critical and judgmental attitudes.

As you read this chart, try to remember times when you have judged others harshly or become self-critical over some rash action you took. Then, answer the following questions:

- Which set of values do I typically follow when I first learn about others' indiscretions?
- How do I evaluate the impact on others of my own insensitive words or thoughtless actions?

"It's interesting that you've used the V-shape," observes Garry as he studies the chart. "The further down the judgmental path I go, the more impossible it becomes to back up and return to that fork in the road where I goofed things up. By then I'm miles away from the compassionate side of myself. The chasm is too deep to jump across, so I'm left there high and dry.

"My trouble is that I don't see the errors of my way soon enough. Insight comes long after all the damage has been done."

Garry has been trying to rebuild trust with his partner, Tim. "Have you made any progress in recognizing the moment when you're first tempted to lay blame and make accusations?" I ask.

Understanding Values	Judgmental Values
Focus on people, relationships	Focus on deeds, actions, situations
Realistic	Perfectionist, idealistic
Understand limitations	Preconceived expectations
Objective, fair	Subjectively biased
Open, flexible	Closed, defensive
Listen without rehearsing	Selective listening
Curious, seek information	Make assumptions, jump to conclusions
Asks clarifying questions	Pronounce, cross-examine
Empathetic, sympathetic, kind	Critical, judgmental, cruel
Honest, straight-forward	Manipulative, devious
Responsible, reliable	Irresponsible reactions
Committed, consistent	Unpredictable, inconsistent
Humble	Arrogantly superior
Dignified	Proud
Tolerant, respectful	Intolerant, disdainful
Optimistic, positive	Pessimistic, negative
Patient	Impatient, impulsive
Use gentle sense of humour	Use sarcasm, put-down humour
Unconditional regard	Conditional regard
Generous	Measured giving, tit-for-tat
Forgiving	Vengeful
Value harmony	Value being "right," one-up
(Positive Feeling Function)	(Negative Thinking Function)

Figure 10.1 Integrity is a choice

In the past it was always Garry who expressed anger and pushed for change. Tim's typical passive-aggressive response was to withdraw into silent resentment. The partners had "danced this dance" once too often, and consequently few problems were ever resolved.

It requires a lot of willpower and discipline to hang onto that brief moment when it's still possible to *choose* how to react. The danger for couples who have a storehouse full of "unfinished business" is that old feelings keep being layered over by fresh ones. The origins of the problem get lost in historical repeats. Then, when self-control goes missing, intimates can be hell-bent for revenge in no time flat.

THE DIFFERENCE BETWEEN FORMING A JUDGMENT AND BEING JUDGMENTAL

Through perception, we automatically gather information and form an opinion about whether someone is potentially good or bad, or something is benign, pleasurable, or dangerous. This natural process is essential for our self-preservation.

What we *chose to do* with our negative evaluations, however, determines whether or not we become judgmental people. If we have integrity, we will treat those we judge with understanding rather than derision or contempt. We will choose to be compassionate in the *way we respond*, rather than be vengeful or vindictive.

The line between stating an opinion and being opinionated is a fine one. Offering an opinion on a particular subject can be a responsible sharing of a personal point of view. To be credible, however, we must be able to support any of our implied criticism or fault-finding with accurate, factual, and defendable data.

To avoid being opinionated, we need to initiate an exchange of views in which each person actively listens and refrains from commenting on whether the other's different opinion is necessarily right or wrong, good or bad.

Negative emotions are extremely powerful forces that mercurially surge up from the depths of our beings to twist us dangerously out of shape. If we're not careful, we can impulsively do the opposite of what would be good, kind, or generous. The *timing* of a response is therefore crucial to integrity. Jumping to conclusions is a foolish choice. It takes time and effort to summon up the self-control necessary to examine a judgmental rebuke through the light of compassionate understanding. As any good lawyer knows, it is always wise to withhold final judgment until all the evidence is in.

It is also risky business to assume that by supporting certain values, we will automatically act with integrity. Next time you're faced with a moral or ethical choice, ask yourself these questions:

- Am I really seeing the "big picture," the complete story?
- Are my own emotional reactions interfering with my ability to remain objective and impartial?
- Am I being naive in thinking that my own personal code of ethics and values are entirely sound, particularly on this subject?

In *Everyday Ethics*, Joshua Halberstam writes that all judgments involve three categories: judgments of oneself, judgments of others, and judgments of situations: "When you judge yourself, your judgments of other people are never too distant. When you judge another person, you base your judgment on your own moral perspective. Before you judge an issue, you always need to canvass your prejudices" (102).

Judging Oneself

Because values shape our identity in the world, we are wise to take the time for periodic *self-evaluation*. To be able to judge ourselves honestly, we must have addressed the existential question, "Who am I, separate and different from others?"

We must also look to the past and question why we've made certain choices but not others.

In the foreword to his play *After the Fall*, Arthur Miller comments on the importance of choice in the never-ending journey towards self-understanding: "Where choice begins, Paradise ends, innocence ends, for what is Paradise but the absence of any need to choose this action?"

He goes on, "The apple cannot be stuck back on the Tree of Knowledge: once we begin to see, we are doomed and challenged to seek the strength to see more, not less."

A *re-evaluation* process takes place when we examine the values we were taught and had modelled for us in childhood. If we discover that our past behaviour has shifted away from societal norms, we may need to revisit some of the mind-bending traumas of our youth in order to understand how these experiences might still be influencing our present attitudes.

The following self-confrontations may kick-start this process.

- Do I presently consider myself a moral person? Do I clearly articulate my personal values and defend my beliefs?
- Do my moral and ethical standards support my spiritual beliefs? In other words, do I say that I value a person or ideal, yet fail to honour this commitment by acting with indifference or malice?
- Do greed and envy or a competitive one-upmanship play a strong role in my choices?

- Is the persona I've created congruent with my real character? Do the things I read, the friends I choose, and the affiliations I make reflect my professed values?

Self-evaluations usually invite obvious comparisons between our own and others' preferences. It's fine to examine our own biases and prejudices, because they reflect a moral perspective for which we are responsible. However, when we take it upon ourselves to measure others' integrity with our own particular measuring stick, we enter dangerous territory indeed.

Our interactions – what we choose to ask or tell others – reveal a great deal about our own character. A group of our couples' friends used to play a party game that I now realize encouraged critical judgment rather than compassion.

Someone in the group was labelled "IT" and sent out of the room. The rest of the group had to assign another person, labelled "X," to be the mystery person whose identity IT must guess upon returning to the room.

When it was their turn to play IT, the more sensitive types asked very superficial, persona-type questions: What kind of dog would person X choose? What watch would X wear? What would X's umbrella look like? What would X's dream house look like? What part of town would that house be in, if X had the opportunity to choose? This line of questioning usually led to quick answers but nervous giggles.

The more aggressive types were out for hilarity. Their invasive questions often amounted to a character assassination, and people were loath to respond. Not surprisingly, this game about other people's choices had a short life. Being IT was a pretty uncomfortable spot to be in, and watching that other person in the room being judged was equally painful.

Observing our everyday conversations, examining what topics we choose and what questions we ask others, as well as our motivation in doing so, can be a helpful self-judging exercise. To help clients assess their progress in developing a stronger conscience, I often ask them to critique their own behaviour, after the fact. How happy were they, for example, with their participation in a conversation?

- Was I interesting and fun to be with, or did I burden the other person with my negativity?
- Did I mainly talk about ideas and issues (Thinking side), or about people and relationships (Feeling side), or a mixture of both?
- Was I trying to get to know that person better, or did I manipulate the conversation back to something that interested me?
- Did I encourage an exchange of views, or was I more interested in getting my own point of view across?

The bottom line of whether judging ourselves is a safe and productive thing to do depends on our level of self-acceptance. Love, not fear, should be our guide on this journey.

Two classic maxims offer guidance for judging oneself. William Shakespeare in *The Tragedy of Hamlet, Prince of Denmark,* has Polonius admonish, "This above all, to thine own self be true." Similarly, Alexander Pope in his *Essay On Man,* Epistle I, adds a cautionary note concerning humility: "Know then thyself, presume not God to scan; the proper study of mankind is man."

Judging Others

People who lie, cheat, or steal care little for the welfare of others. Their focus is on protecting their own self-serving interests, not on the emotional or financial cost to us, their victims. However, by judging their actions as despicable or outrageous, we move into a "we-they" mentality.

Too often we dismiss the individual behind the crime and thereby ignore human frailty in general. To avoid doing this, we need to take the next step and wonder, "Why does so-and-so do what he does?"

This decision to put energy into understanding someone or something is likely pre-determined by our own level of tolerance and humility. Have we developed the admirable ability to learn from life's lessons, forgive, and then move on?

Personal bias must be accounted for whenever we formulate an opinion based on experiential data – what we actually observe, hear, or read. Too often our perceptions are narrowly filtered through the prism of our own history, family influences, and cultural norms and habits. The conclusions we reach cannot help but be tainted by these projections.

Another important factor in judging others is the ever-present danger of assuming that we actually *know* what someone else is thinking or feeling. In fact, integrity is missing whenever people second-guess others. The arrogant remark, "I know you better than you know yourself!" illustrates this presumption well. Respect is rarely present when someone else tells us what we think or feel – or worse still, what we *should* think or feel.

A series of psychological experiments during the 1960s and early 1970s attempted to teach students to guess what others were feeling so that they could act as judges. Despite the use of clever designs and techniques to convey certain feelings through pictures, actors, and real situations, the studies were eventually abandoned because researchers could not even establish a 35 per cent reliability score (Krech et al.). The obvious implication is that an "educated guess" about what others are feeling or thinking is likely to be wrong about 65 per cent of the time! It is our version of reality, not theirs.

By making it a practice to *always ask questions rather than make assumptions*, we foster peer relationships in which both parties honour their commonalities *and* differences. We choose to actively listen and act as a sounding board when someone is telling us about a personal problem. If we don't understand something, we can ask clarifying questions.

We fine-tune our integrity each time we refrain from giving others advice, especially about a personal matter. People need to *own* their own solutions in order to build their self-esteem.

Even if the topic of discussion is an impersonal one, it is still that person's issue to solve. If we have information on the subject that might be helpful, we need to ask for permission *before* we offer it unsolicited. Such a courtesy shows respect and builds trust.

Sometimes, conversely, the *failure* to judge others can be perceived as patronizing and condescending. This happens when we refuse to take seriously what someone else has said.

Joshua Halberstam warns us to be aware of making excuses for others' poor behaviour: "When we excuse someone for an action, we place the blame on some cause other than his character" (*Everyday Ethics*, 128). Halberstam adds, "We want people to hold us responsible for what we do, even if that means ticking them off" (126). In other words, people often find anger preferable to pity.

Judging Issues

Do your own moral judgments on issues of the day simply reflect matters of personal taste or preference, or are they founded on wisely reasoned thinking that has been tempered by compassion? Do the rules and regulations you uphold remain static, or are they flexible enough to reflect evolving cultural traditions and ethical practices?

Businesses can also encounter difficulties when they introduce change on moral grounds. You may have faced problems in your workplace as efforts are made to correct past wrongs.

Eric's firm now has a policy of zero tolerance for any discrimination in the workplace. Much thought has gone into developing ethical and moral guidelines that abide by current legislation.

At a meeting one day, the chief executive officer brings up what turns out to be a troubling matter. His seventy-year-old aunt is not comfortable dealing with a young female sales consultant, and the CEO wants his aunt to see an older male counterpart instead. This breaches new policy, and an uneasy silence hangs over the conference room. No one confronts the boss.

As the ethics officer of this company, Eric is faced with an obvious dilemma. He leaves the room with his stomach churning and unsettling thoughts swirling around in his head. He ponders: "Where does this leave all the hard-won victories my committee has gained for employees' rights? What precisely is *my* responsibility at this point?"

His CEO is a man with a well-earned reputation for not tolerating challenges to his authority. In this instance, the boss is championing the rights of the customer over the staff and opening the door to further discrimination. Eric understands only too well that his job may be on the line if he takes a strong stand in defence of the rights of employees. As he struggles with his conscience, he wonders if the board will support him, should he need to make public the boss's request for an exception to the rule.

The status quo is clearly shaken whenever new rules are set in motion that challenge unethical practices. Carving out standards of conduct that honour *revised* belief systems is never easy. "What was" must give way to "what is" as tough questions need to be addressed and new procedures enforced. Practicalities dictate, of course, that newly conceived policies must hold up over time.

As in Eric's case, upholding integrity may come at a cost. If he is wise, he will stick to the issue at hand and keep personality differences and his own ego separate and apart.

Having had time to reflect, Eric tells me that he has some empathy for his boss's wish to placate his aunt. Eric knows his own Shadow well enough by now to understand the temptation to play a Mr Nice Guy role rather than do what is right. But he has decided to stick to the real issue, the upholding of company policy. He plans to consult with his team to re-evaluate *how* the policies can actually be upheld in daily practice, and what is at stake should any exceptions be granted. He won't let himself be swayed by pressure, and knows he must be on guard against his boss's persistent need to hammer away until he gets his own way.

Eric seems pleased that this time he conquered his knee-jerk tendency to ignore caution and respond too quickly. His touchy oversensitivity in the past only encouraged his judgmental attitude. I share my own insight with him about how I attempt to keep on the path of understanding. As a psychologist, I regularly encounter upset, angry people and must remind myself that the underlying motivation for anger is fear. I lay the groundwork for future questioning by pondering why someone's response is so extreme, and what present or even past circumstances might be threatening his or her security. Later on, when that person is less agitated and more able to listen and respond, I may discover the *real* answers to these queries.

CHOOSING THE PATH
OF UNDERSTANDING

Integrity is built up, or torn down, one step at a time. It's therefore important to know just how choosing the path of understanding protects integrity. Let's look at your reaction to this all-too-familiar, sad tale.

Cynthia, a bright, thirty-eight year old accountant, is perched on the edge of her chair, clearly in deep distress. "Is this about a business situation, or a personal matter?" I enquire.

As it turns out, Cynthia has allowed her wilful nature to run roughshod over her self-professed intention to maintain high standards. She has become romantically involved with her boss, an older, married man with four children. After discovering the affair, the boss's wife confronted Cynthia in an angry and heated telephone exchange.

Not only is Cynthia still emotionally distraught by the wife's call, but yesterday her boss suggested that she quietly resign so *his* reputation wouldn't be tarnished by a public scandal. "He loves me, *but.*"

If your reaction to this story takes a judgmental approach, you might be thinking: "She couldn't be very bright to let herself be seduced by such a scoundrel!" Or, "For heaven's sake, doesn't this lady *think?*"

If your reaction follows an understanding path, you might be wondering how Cynthia got herself into this mess in the first place. What did the boss tell her about his marital status? Why did she let their attraction blossom into an affair? Was she anxious to find a partner soon because she desperately wants children? Only Cynthia knows the truth.

Monitoring our typical reactions to similar tales can be a helpful self-exploration. What do the questions we ask ourselves tell us about our own integrity?

- Does hearing frequent stories about infidelity, physical and sexual abuse, cheating, theft, fraud, rape, or murder diminish or strengthen my moral position?
- Which transgressions trouble me the most?
- How does learning about another's loss of integrity affect my behaviour towards that person?
- Does my opinion shift if the news concerns a leading politician, a well-known professional, or a popular sports figure?
- Will I vote for this individual in the next election in spite of the reported scandal?
- Will I continue to cheer on that sports hero at the next event?
- Will I still go to my dentist or doctor or support my clergy when there are unsubstantiated rumours flying about?

Would your response and actions be the same or different if the story was closer to home?

- How might I react if the wrongdoing involved a family member, friend, or colleague?
- Would I remain loyal to a colleague so charged?
- Would I neglect to call or just stop seeing a friend?
- Would I remain in my marriage if my spouse was unfaithful or committed some fraudulent act at work?

If we tend to be judgmental, our opinions will be relatively clear cut. We make a decision one way or the other; case dismissed. However, if we've chosen the understanding path, especially when the story involves us personally, nothing is simple. Most moral and ethical problems are characteristically complex, so we need to take time to reflect in depth. It may or may not be appropriate for us to ask questions of the parties involved. In the case of an impersonal news story, we often need more facts or historical data from a number of reliable sources *before* finalizing our conclusions.

Whenever our choices reflect an up-down, black-white, right-wrong bias, the problems seem to multiply. Think of the key character traits of integrity – honesty, sympathy, empathy, compassion, fairness, self-control and duty – and consider what happens to them when we express a judgmental view.

Honesty is false whenever we make judgments without first considering *all* the available information. A closed mind is highly selective.

Sympathy, empathy, and compassion receive scant attention when we focus narrowly on making critical judgments. Declarations of blame that push harsh views upon reluctant ears make a travesty of unconditional regard.

Fairness comes off poorly when we allow prejudice, bias, and intolerance to co-exist. Arrogance breeds irresponsible views, and we may make statements that are accusatory, inconsistent, or false, only confusing the listener. It is not fair to attack another's viewpoint or cross-examine with the sole intent of proving the other person wrong.

Self-control can get swallowed up in outrage. When we are judgmental, we become defensive and "protest too much." Our unconsidered tit-for-tat retorts can be vengeful. We may find ourselves using sarcasm to put others down.

Duty is absent when we make cruel judgments that diminish others' worth. Duty always concerns itself with the welfare and dignity of others.

INTERNALIZING VALUES

If our opinions and actions are to be consistent and predictable, we need to possess a strong core of inner values.

Some twenty years ago, I devised a problem-solving approach I call Internalizing. This process teaches people to gather information from *both* the Feeling and Thinking problem-solving functions to ensure that their personal judgments are not only intelligent but also wise and compassionate.[1] I tell my clients that the process of learning to Internalize is the most important that I will ever teach them.

The Internalizing process encourages us to take *full* responsibility for our reactions and subsequent responses. When we learn to establish clear ego boundaries, we can state what we feel and think without being invasive or controlling. Our task is to understand our own reactions, not to second-guess or project our views onto others.

EXTERNAL FRAME OF REFERENCE

Externalizers are people who have developed an external frame of reference. They hold values and beliefs that are easily swayed, especially by their unique view of what others expect. These "reactors" have learned early on to "use whatever works."

Usually Externalizers come from families where love was conditional and approval was meted out for accomplishments, not for character traits such as sensitivity or kindness. Some played the "good kid" role in the family and tried too hard to please. More manipulative types learned to second-guess what others wanted and then shifted their words and actions accordingly.

Neither role encourages integrity, because the personal values of these people fluctuate depending on the pragmatics of their situation or personal needs.

---

1 A more thorough explanation may be found in my book, *The Balancing Act: Rediscovering Your Feelings.*

Externalizers tend to process information in the following manner. When something happens, the Thinking function automatically kicks in to anticipate another person's possible reactions. Based on this *projection*, Externalizers offer a calculated, "appropriate" response. But by focusing on external cues, they neglect to listen to their own gut feelings and inner wisdom about what is right. They rarely ask questions or seek out information from those they wish to please. Instead, they transform their projected ideas into "valid" opinions.

Because their Thinking function works overtime, Externalizers have a tendency to be "fixers" who freely problem-solve for others and tell people what they should and shouldn't do. Thinking's hierarchical structure naturally encourages this one-up position.

This is just one of the negative properties of Thinking that dominates this process. Feeling's other-directed compassion doesn't stand a chance. Thus, integrity is slowly distorted by pragmatism.

INTERNAL FRAME OF REFERENCE

Internalizers are focused on understanding their *own* reactions, not on judging or "fixing" someone else. Their inner values strongly influence what these folks choose to say or do in response to another's actions. They formulate their opinions by using both Feeling and Thinking problem-solving functions to inform their judgment.

Internalizers are *proactive* rather than reactive. They must learn how they feel and what they think and be in control of their emotions so that they can articulate their opinions clearly and succinctly. They develop the willpower to refrain from problem-solving until their internal cues are processed and they have sought out pertinent information from external sources.

How We Feel

To know how we feel, we must be in touch with our feelings and be able to name and identify them. Obviously, this task is more difficult for people whose Thinking is dominant. As well, there are other reasons why the Feeling function may have been repressed at an early stage of development.

Much of the work I do as a clinical psychologist involves the difficult task of helping people get back in touch with their feelings through their bodies. The brain receives messages through the body's muscles and nerve endings that signal that a certain emotional response has occurred. By learning to make these signals conscious, we can quickly "know" how we feel and be able to label and differentiate the feeling by calling it, for example, "fear," or "sadness."

We can gather further clues through an awareness of our energy levels and body positions.

What We Think

To understand our own reactions to someone or something, we use an analytical thinking process. We must seek out answers to certain questions:

1 *What* just happened?
2 *Who* said what?
3 And more exactly, s*pecifically* what am I reacting to in this situation?

We can unearth unconscious material by asking an additional question:

4 Am I *overreacting* or acting impulsively because of a layering of old feelings over my present ones?

Typically, overreactions are a sign that our past feelings are rising to the surface and compounding our present reaction. When old memories heighten our responses, the very mention of some subject can tap into an Achilles heel, a vulnerability that multiplies stress.

For example, a couple may have had numerous arguments over the years about how their money is spent. When they have to make a joint decision about some purchase, both parties are immediately on the defensive. As blood pressures soar, anger mounts, and Mount Vesuvius erupts.

It takes much discipline to ask ourselves these questions, to puzzle over why we may be fuzzy about certain details or why we yelled at someone and said something totally out of character.

Self-Control

As Internalizers, we have to be willing to delay problem-solving until we understand the reasons for our own reaction and feel in control of our emotions. Integrity requires us to gather accurate and authentic evidence *before* responding.

We must make a gut-level judgment about whether or not we are in enough control to communicate without crossing the ego boundary and telling others what to do. Feedback from our body about our stress level helps us make this decision. If we find ourselves still confused or conflicted, it is time to reschedule.

Rescheduling

Rescheduling is an important process in maintaining integrity. It allows us to state the reason for the postponement with phrases such as "I'm too confused to think clearly right now. I need to take some time to think this through and then get back to you." Or, "I'm just too angry to make any sense out of this. I need to calm myself down before we resume our talk."

Both parties then arrange a mutually acceptable time for further dialogue when they are more relaxed and better able to listen.

Calming techniques such as meditation and prayer, and the use of humour and visualizations, are helpful tools to restore equilibrium. The faster we are able to regain control, the more effective communicators we'll become.

Communicating Using the "I" Message

The "I" statement is a brief, non-controlling communication describing our reaction. First we state how we feel, and then what we think, and then, if it is appropriate, how our needs may have been affected.

No judgment of the other person should be involved, only a simple reference to what it was that initially triggered our response. If we begin our description by using Feeling's gracious language and conciliatory tone of voice, the other person is less likely to become defensive.

The following statement uses the "I" message to ask for more information: "I'm feeling uncomfortable about agreeing to your plans for the weekend. Would you please tell me a bit more about what you had in mind and who is going to be involved?"

Once the request has been made, the other person must be left free to respond in any way he or she chooses. That choice may or may not be to our liking, but we must not resort to pressure or manipulation.

The process of communicating without controlling makes it much easier to resolve "unfinished business." Having been assertive and spoken up for ourselves, we will have less need to hold a grudge.

Sometimes other people will choose not to take part in solving differences of opinion with us. We may have to agree to disagree and leave some time for reflection and healing. It's easier to do this if we remain open and don't take differences of opinion personally.

Integrity blossoms in the atmosphere that Internalizing creates. Here is a summary of some of its advantages:

- Our decisions are informed by judgments that are gathered from *both* compassionate feeling and well-thought out analysis.
- We are proactive rather than reactive in seeking solutions. Our actions are directed by an inner core of solid values.
- We respectfully ask questions to gain more information. There is no need to put our own "spin" on things because we are not trying to influence others to change their minds.
- We develop the willpower to *think twice* before we speak and to reschedule when we find ourselves overreacting.
- We take full responsibility for all our actions *and* reactions within a relationship and avoid blaming others. We willingly share the responsibility for finding solutions to troublesome problems.
- We are flexible and open to new challenges and truths, but our beliefs and morality are not easily swayed.

When all is said and done, self-control and taking personal responsibility for our own opinions and actions is what integrity is all about – the uncompromising commitment to honour moral, spiritual, and artistic values and principles.

The health of integrity in our society, in the family, and in the workplace depends on the moral and ethical choices we make each day. Let's look at some of the ways we can make a difference!

11

Safeguarding Integrity

You can't, in sound morals, condemn a man for taking care of his own
integrity. It is his clear duty.

> Joseph Conrad, *A Personal Record*

In *A Personal Record,* Joseph Conrad stresses the role of the individual's conscience in safeguarding integrity: "In that interior world
where his thought and his emotions go seeking for the experience
of imagined adventures, there are no policemen, no law, no pressure of circumstance or dread of opinion to keep him within
bounds. Who then is going to say Nay to his temptations if not his
conscience?"

HAS INTEGRITY DIED?

What has happened to good old-fashioned morality and ethics, the
public face of private integrity? There's rarely a day goes by that
someone else with supposedly high moral credentials doesn't fall
from grace.

The present state of integrity was the subject of an interview with
Major Barry Armstrong, retiring chief surgeon at the National
Defence Military Centre in Ottawa, Armstrong was the man who
blew the whistle in the infamous Somalia inquiry into the murder
of a young man by Canadian soldiers. Columnist Anthony Jenkins
in the *Globe and Mail* asked him the significant question, "Has integrity died?"

Major Armstrong's optimistic reply was reassuring. "Absolutely
not! It's alive and well ... It is cultured, nurtured, shaped and
tended. If we don't make some effort, each of us within our self,
then perhaps our personal integrity could wither, but I don't think
it takes many people of integrity to make a society that has integrity.

All it takes is one honest man. I had no idea I had any developed ethics or integrity. I'm an ordinary person forced by circumstances to take a strong moral stand."

ROLE MODELS FOR INTEGRITY

It is important to ask ourselves whether we truly appreciate the people in our own lives who possess this admirable trait. Most of the people I interviewed for this book chose quite ordinary people as their role models. "You never know with public figures what they're really like in private," I was often told.

William, a public-relations lawyer, spoke about being acutely aware of the inner glow of a fellow university student from thirty years ago: "Al never wore his honesty like clothing, but it was always there. It was understated, unstated, in fact, but it was his essence; and it shone all the more brightly because it was so automatic to him.

"He couldn't hurt and he couldn't lie. He accepted others and me at face value – without qualification, judgment or guile. And even though my own virtue paled by comparison and left me a little ashamed, I never felt resentful of this gap because I knew its existence never would have occurred to him for a moment."

William's second choice was a successful executive with high principles for whom he did some legal work over several years. This gentleman evoked the same feelings in William that Al had, years earlier:

Max had exacting standards and high expectations of others, too high and inflexible sometimes. But again, like Al, his honesty was palpable, and it came from a place in him far deeper than reflex. He never talked about the importance of integrity in business; it was the only way he knew. Doing otherwise would not have entered his mind. That reality created an almost visible aura around him which others could easily see.

For both Al and Max, honesty was beyond choice. It was inherent. Never cheap gossip, unkind criticism, the white lie, or the selfish but hurtful choice. And never preaching. They taught in the most effective way of all, by example. When I am living on my more jaded side, these men seem at times almost naive. But they weren't. Their integrity just rings so true even today because it existed at a higher level of being.

William's two role models have what I call *integrated* integrity. We can count ourselves lucky if we have been influenced by people with such character. Even though they may have entered our lives only briefly, they leave an impression that remains forever.

"A serene presence and calmness" are qualities Teresa, a young homemaker, ascribes to a good friend who listened to her complaints about her own attention-demanding son: "She listened to me intently, and didn't give me even one piece of advice. Instead she agreed, confirmed, and talked about some of her related experiences. Those words were coming straight from her heart, and I never felt that they were meant to compare or make my trials less important than hers. I also knew that if I asked her to keep a matter private, she definitely would.

"I know I can count on her to be kind and truthful because she has such a powerful sense of values. It's awesome!"

For these role models, integrity is no longer an issue. They obviously made significant choices a long time ago. But let's not be fooled by what we view as their seemingly effortless maturity.

At some time or other, our role models had to learn to value the traits of self-control and duty and the spirit of generosity. Many have an underlying spirituality and grace that shines through their acts of kindness. They've found a good balance between individual rights and freedom and joint responsibility to family and the wider community.

THE LESSONS WE TEACH

Safeguarding integrity in our own families is an awesome responsibility. Some good advice for parents is spelled out in the lyrics for Stephen Sondheim and James Lapine's insightful musical, *Into the Woods*. In RCA Victor's original cast recording, the newly transformed witch warns us:

Careful the things you say,
Children will listen.
Careful the things you do,
Children will see
And learn.

Children may not obey,
But children will listen.

Children will look to you
For which way to turn,
To learn what to be.

Careful before you say,
"Listen to me."
Children will listen.

The chorus joins in the final song:

Into the woods
You have to grope,
But that's the way
You learn to cope.

Into the woods
To find there's hope
Of getting through the journey.

Moral lessons children learn at early stages of development have a profound effect on them, even though the wisdom acquired may not be acknowledged until later in life.

A strict adherence to the rules and etiquette of sport is but one way to teach integrity. In *Final Rounds: A Father, A Son, the Golf Journey of a Lifetime*, golf writer James Dodson tells how he discovered much about himself when he took his dying father to several famous courses in the British Isles for one last glorious golf holiday.

James's father, Brax Dodson, considered golf a character-builder that teaches valuable lessons about oneself, about others, and indeed about the world. He was a stickler for the rules of golf, which he truly believed to be as essential as oxygen.

As a teenager, James hated the gentle but firm "rulebook Elijah," as he coined the cornball philosopher side of his father. Brax's rules were succinct: "You marked your ball properly; you fixed dents in the green; you putted in turn; you offered to tend the pin; you congratulated an opponent on a good shot." Through golf etiquette, he taught his son consideration, thoughtfulness, and a respect for rules and regulations.

A traumatic lesson occurred early on when James slammed his putter into the green because he had missed a short putt. Brax insisted that his son leave the course immediately. James was to report to the pro, Aubrey Apple, and apologize. After identifying James as Brax Dodson's kid, Apple reportedly said, "Anybody who beats up my golf greens is a little shit. We don't need any little shits out here." He banned this particular "Valley Rat," as the pro called young golf enthusiasts, from the course for two weeks. James recalled his angst: "This verdict was torture, like a death sentence" (8–9).

Their final golf journey, an act of love between father and son, was a testament to the wisdom that tough love offers when it is combined with a reverence for the humane and sensitive rules of life.

SAFEGUARDING INTEGRITY FOR THE FUTURE

Our society in general needs to make integrity the cornerstone of a visionary movement to rebuild a fresh reference for universal truth, love, and human dignity.

As citizens, we want our schools to teach healthy character development, and we want our institutions to support and reinforce sound moral values and laws. Whistle-blowers in the workplace need our protection, instead of being scapegoated as so often happens.

At home we have the privilege and duty to pass along this priceless legacy to our children, from the "terrible twos" to the angst-ridden years of adolescence. Without guiding principles, the turbulent years of rebellious searching can end badly. It's our job to help those in our care cope and survive whatever is out there "in the woods."

As Michael Ignatieff reminds us in *The Rights Revolution*, "Parents needn't be heroes – moral or otherwise. Nor should they be friends. They should be parents" (108). If wage and time pressures "deplete the emotional reserves of family life," he warns, "children are less likely to learn the values on which the larger society depends." Children who are afraid of their parents and do not learn to trust or love will turn into aggressive and selfish adults (91).

Beliefs and Values

At the heart of integrity is what each of us *personally chooses to believe in.* However, just as compassion must be accompanied by action, parental beliefs and values need to be clearly expressed, modelled, and firmly upheld if they are to have a lasting impact on young minds.

Parents would no doubt be most upset if someone accused them of not leaving their children well cared for financially, yet they neglect the duty of leaving their children morally prepared for life.

Parents need to express their personal views on moral issues to their children. But they cannot stop there. They need to take advantage of opportunities to *exchange* ideas, and make integrity relevant to everyday matters. They might ask for a child's opinion about a current news story that raises an ethical issue. They need to take care not to lecture but simply listen. Children need to feel free to evolve their own beliefs about doing the right thing.

If children's views diverge widely from the norm, they should be encouraged to discuss their ideas with a peer, a sibling, or some other adult. The act of having to articulate, support, and defend an idea helps refine a belief. Even radical ideas can expose hypocrisy.

It is important for parents to teach the idea of consensus, that there are commonly held values that support harmonious togetherness. However, there will always be different and valid ideas that question those firmly held beliefs.

Childhood naivety needs to be challenged by the idea of adversity, that life is both difficult and rewarding. Overprotective parenting distorts this perception and falsifies reality.

Children deserve to hear that belief systems are precious, and often costly, that the personal freedom necessary to choose integrity will always be subject to threats from the outside – from ideologies gone terribly wrong. By sitting down together and watching news coverage of conflicts around the world, parents can initiate conversations about how beliefs and values are misused to foster terrorism and other evils.

Children love being read morality tales, which coincidently teach the importance of willpower, of *not* giving in to the lure of instant gratification or greedy gain. Parents can choose inspirational movies or plays for the family in which ordinary people strive for decency and human values, despite being left troubled and deeply scarred by trauma and chaos.

The question "How do you think you would have handled that situation?" might encourage a child's compassionate identification with the sufferer's plight.

Children should be encouraged to support the causes of popular heroes who have used their will to overcome physical limitations. They might join in the Terry Fox run for cancer research or have the opportunity to give part of their allowance to support a charity such as the fund for spinal cord injury research established by the late actor Christopher Reeves.

H.J. Blackham describes this will to overcome adversity in his introduction to *Reality, Man and Existence*: "Human reality, then, is constituted by an ability to separate itself from what is there and to project itself beyond what is there; unlike things, which are and remain solely what they are in the world. I am not my life, my fate. Or, rather, I am not wholly that. I can turn from my actualities to my potentialities, and it is then that I encounter myself" (5).

Respect for Rules, Regulations, and Laws

Underlying established rules and traditions are sound values that consider the common good. Parents who break rules plant the seeds in their watchful children for future misdemeanours or wilful action. Young couples caught up in the romantic phase of courting unfortunately often neglect to explore the mutuality of their beliefs and standards. When it comes time to teach their children values, they may discover glaring differences.

Clarity is important, so parents must watch out for mixed messages. If children are to learn that respecting laws is a personal duty, their parents' words and actions must match.

On the way to school the "Do as I say, but not as I do" type of parent tells his children to always obey stop signs while he drives above the speed limit and tailgates the car ahead. When his alarmed wife protests, he retaliates. He just can't tolerate being told what to do. "If you weren't such a nagging fuss-budget, I could stay calm and drive more slowly," he fumes.

The children in the back seat soak all this up and grow anxious. The lesson they learn in this heated exchange is not about respecting traffic laws.

Predictability provides security. If parents are weak in their resolve to follow through on their beliefs, children can't be expected to take values seriously. But a discussion with a child in which a parent admits ambivalence or difficulty in deciding what is the *right* thing to do can be a mutually beneficial exercise.

Ask your child to comment on the parent's action in the following situation.

A ten-year old boy named Tyler tells his mother he's going to sneak into the fairground with his buddy. "Well, we're going to stand in line to get our tickets," Mom chimes in. "You decide what you're going to do."

Tyler manages to slip in the back way and meets his parents halfway through the show. Later, feeling pangs of guilt, he comes up to his mother looking kind of miserable. "Can I have your ticket stub, Mom?" he pleads.

This mom gave in to her son and consequently watered down her resolve to foster honesty. A reply such as: "That wouldn't be right if I gave you my stub" would have maintained a consistency of action. Tyler would learn that rights come with responsibilities.

Guidance is necessary, because children need limits and rules. The laissez-faire attitude of permissive parents can leave youngsters feeling adrift and emotionally overwhelmed. "Don't rock the boat" becomes their motto.

In Jeanette's family, contentious issues were never discussed. "I guess I was just expected to know!" was her conclusion. She was bound that this wouldn't happen to her children. One day her fourteen-year old daughter Samantha was completing a purchase ahead of Jeanette in the drug store line-up.

Jeanette waited until she was outside the store before speaking to Sam. "Do you realize that the clerk gave you two dollars too much change?"

"Ah, Mom, it's only a toonie!" Sam rationalized.

"Well, dear, I take this kind of thing quite seriously. I want to treat other people fairly. That poor gal probably has to make up any shortfalls. Two dollars is two dollars! It's your decision, Sam! When I'm faced with a dilemma like this, I sometimes find it helpful to talk it over with someone else."

At a later time, Jeanette may wish to tell Sam about how difficult it was for her *not* to be able to talk over problems with her parents. In the immediate situation, however, that would come across as an unwelcome lecture. After all, talking it over is ultimately Samantha's choice, not Jeanette's.

To summarize, consider the following guidelines when choosing what to say to children, and how to say it.

- Briefly state your opinion, along with the beliefs or values behind your reasoning. Any digression that takes the focus away from the topic will only confuse your child.
- Be aware that young children are concrete in their thinking, at least until abstract thinking develops around the ages of seven or eight. Therefore, keep your language simple and avoid concepts that are beyond your child's ability to comprehend.
- Ask children to explain the reasons for their choices or ambivalence. Listen carefully, and don't interrupt unless you can't follow their logic.
- When moral issues are raised in the media, ask your children for their opinions about a person, an action, or an issue. This will help them formalize their own beliefs about complex moral dilemmas.

PRACTICES AND BELIEFS IN THE WORKPLACE

The more impersonal the work setting, the more danger there is that the lack of group loyalty and the sense of belonging and duty will encourage a mix of isolation, alienation, and greedy self-interest.

Workaholics thrive in this impersonal world because intimacy might threaten their hold on power. No wonder we are witnessing widespread corporate fraud and accounting scandals – added proof that integrity is indeed in trouble in our society.

Although prohibiting e-mails has been suggested as a stress-reduction solution in the workplace, this action might only increase the anxiety of chronic workaholics who get stressed out by too many on-going face-to-face encounters with colleagues outside their immediate circle.

In today's workplace, intensity and efficiency are fast replacing the respectful comradeship, mutual trust, and compassionate intimacy so necessary for meaningful professional relationships. After all, one has to truly care about people in order to treat them well.

To safeguard integrity in the workplace, we need to protest and challenge a short-sighted but popular trend in business organizations. In a process sometimes called "hoteling," flexible field offices are set up in which employees do much of their work on e-mail, at home or on the road. Office space is booked as needed, and people come and go. This model champions cost-effective efficiency.

In the long run, however, loyalty and intimacy in the workplace suffer. Logistically, it is hard to find and sustain a mutually agreeable time for people to work together on projects. The human element of watching expressions and intuiting body language is missing, as is the companionship of talking over current affairs, sports scores, or personal problems.

People need a strong sense of belonging in order to build group loyalty. Those tempted to cheat or lie to workmates or bosses are far less likely to do so if they have to face these people daily.

Intimacy in the workplace is of special interest to Max De Pree, a businessman whose furniture-making company was chosen by *Fortune* magazine as one of the hundred best companies to work for in America. In *Leadership Is an Art*, De Pree suggests that beliefs are connected to intimacy and should come before policies, standards, or practices. A real intimacy with work itself adds value to an organization by deepening each employee's personal involvement and accountability.

"Intimacy is the experience of ownership," De Pree adds. The personality of the business operator must fit the job if this feeling of ownership is to flourish.

Leaders who encumber workers rather than empower them betray this intimacy. Organizational structures are needed that rise above a focus on methodology and quantification. People need road maps that enable them to work together cooperatively.

In De Pree's view, the enemies of group intimacy are "politics, short-term measurements, arrogance, superficiality, and an orientation toward self rather than toward the good of the group" (55–6).

Adrian Gostick and Dana Telford in *The Integrity Advantage* cite the view of Harvard professor Joe Badaracco that people with integrity are "quiet leaders: They don't spearhead large-scale ethical crusades. They right – or prevent – moral wrongs in the workplace inconspicuously and usually without casualties" (66). Their extraordinary achievements are in large measure due to their modesty and restraint.

Use integrity's core values to foster group intimacy and humility.

- Refuse to get caught up in destructive power struggles. Try to stay focused on understanding the issues rather than judging the warring factions or criticizing someone's personality.
- It benefits everyone on the job if you make a long-term commitment to honour and support your co-workers. Recognize your own limitations with humility, and take the time to praise a colleague's valuable ideas and special talents.
- Possess enough savvy to take a task seriously but not your own importance.

Business ethics remains a hot topic today because the public is greatly alarmed about the absence of responsible truth telling, the growing need of protection for both people and property, and the serious concern for the environment and the survival of life on this planet as we now know it.

INTEGRATED INTEGRITY:
BEYOND CHOICE

We strengthen our character each time our conscience and will-power win out over temptation and perfectionistic idealism.

Be true to the Self. Honest self-reflection is necessary for emotional stability and peace of mind. To achieve self-acceptance is to accept the wisdom that the whole is the sum of its parts. Transformation is possible only if we affirm our strengths and, equally, embrace our weaknesses.

The English poet and engraver William Blake suffered a lifetime of insecurity because he failed to recognize that his greatness lay in having experienced long-forgotten sufferings and buried childhood fears. Blake's biographer, Peter Ackroyd, suggests that this genius "might not have wanted to come too close to himself, in case he did not care for what he found there ... That is why he felt the pressing need to express himself and yet at the same time to frame doubts about the nature of that expression by making it ambiguous, satirical or impersonal" (154–5).

Blake was making use of dissociation to *distance* himself from the painful reality of his youth.

In my clinical practice, when clients are ready to challenge their dark side, I ask them to zero in on one of their most troublesome traits. Arrogance, controlling, insensitivity, selfishness and dishonesty seem to be popular choices.

If someone pinpoints insensitivity, for example, the next step involves a reality-testing exercise. I ask the person to describe in writing five separate occasions when he or she was insensitive. Each situation, whether long past or current, must involve a different person. The content of these stories form the basis for our exploration.

By our brainstorming together to establish more appropriate ways of reacting and responding verbally, clients gain insight into how they sabotage their integrity. Their confidence builds as they figure out better ways to resolve "unfinished business." This Achilles heel seems less daunting as new behaviours slowly begin to feel more natural.

A variation of this exercise is to strengthen one of our positive traits, be it honesty, sympathy, empathy, compassion, fairness, self-control or duty. I tell my clients, "Each time you walk away from an unsatisfactory conversation or awkward encounter, critique your own participation. Begin by asking yourself how you could have acted in a more responsible or compassionate manner."

Some conscience-raising queries follow.

- What words would have helped me be more gracious or diplomatic?
- How could I be more clear in expressing my ideas?
- What do I need to do to remind myself to ask for others' viewpoints?
- How could I concentrate on being patient while waiting for a reply?
- Was I proactive in seeking a solution, or did I just quickly react?

Strive for balance. Fortunately, the psyche has a wonderful built-in homeostatic mechanism that signals the need for correction when we get seriously out of balance. Anxiety, obsession, and depression are clear warning signals. It's time to do some growing.

Intensity often signals a talent being too narrowly pursued. Someone may soar professionally, yet live a life of quiet desperation. The identity of many gifted artists, writers, musicians, and sports figures is hopelessly intertwined with their work. As perfectionism takes its toll, these famed individuals become their persona, and the Self disappears. We can learn much about ourselves from their stories.

World renowned pianist Glenn Gould was consumed by his creative genius and tortured by the extreme anxiety that obsessive-compulsive behaviours elicit. Eventually he could no longer cope with the pressures of live performances. Anyone who has seen Francois Girard's film *Thirty-Two Short Films about Glenn Gould* cannot help but be struck by Gould's desperate need of personal support from others, at any time of day or night. His own psychic strength was swallowed up when the demands of his career placed an unsupportable drain on his energy. His damaged psyche could no longer sustain him, either psychologically or physically.

Clearly, creativity and genius are not enough to guarantee integrity, an honouring of the Self. The secret lies in knowing how to soar, while at the same time managing to keep one's feet firmly anchored in reality.

The opening words of Robert Browning's poem, "Andrea del Sarto" – "Ah, but a man's reach should exceed his grasp, / Or what's a heaven for?" – came to mind as I listened to Radio Australia early one morning. A blind man was talking to an interviewer about taking flying lessons – one of the many such adventures he had pursued in order to lead a full life.

I'm sure that his obstinate drive must inspire other disabled people to take risks. Yet I wondered whether his brave courage sometimes came at the expense of the significant people in his life who helped him cope day to day. It would be difficult to find a fine balance.

The welfare of others is of prime importance for integrity. The psyche moves towards balance when intensity is replaced by a fresh sense of pleasure and satisfaction because we've gone out of our way to do something kind or helpful. We feel euphoric when our spirituality is deepened by an act of love. Maturity comes when we stretch our potential to help others by using hitherto hidden gifts.

In workshops on the topic of living a balanced life, I often ask my audience to draw a large circle on a page. They are to divide up this Energy Wheel, as I call it, and proportion each of the sections to represent where their time and energy was spent in the past week. They are left free to name the sections, but work, spouse, children, friends, hobbies, spirituality, community service are some obvious choices. Needless to say, this is usually an eye-opener, as all too often the work section leaves little room for anything or anybody else.

Celebrate the day when you can honestly say that you feel more balanced! You're making headway on transforming your faults, and you're giving away your gifts, no strings attached.

Try this self-confrontation to rate your progress towards a more balanced psyche:

- Are my beliefs and values sound, or do I still have to struggle hard not to give in to temptations?
- Where does my stability come from? Do I have an integrated core of values, or am I still allowing external forces to influence my reactions?
- Do I make an effort to understand why someone has lost his or her integrity? Does this strengthen my own resolve, or lessen it because "what's the point if others don't seem to care?"
- Do I have a clear sense of identity, separate and apart from what I do work-wise? Are my energies equitably divided so that my nurturing Being-side is powerful enough to withstand pressure from my performance-driven persona?
- Do I seek out people with integrity as role models, or am I influenced more by those who have charisma, power, and wealth?
- Is my integrity more evident at work or at home?

Be appreciative of what is. The Chinese have a symbol that is the same for both opportunity and chaos. Temptation can be equally seductive in both scenarios. One of the best ways to resist temptation and keep on the straight and narrow path is to be truly appreciative of what we already have, as well as what we are.

Integrity keeps its gratitude intact. Working with workaholics and their families all these years, I've been struck by what appears to be the workaholic's total lack of appreciation. Sadly, the spouse is *expected* to be supportive but receives no gratitude or emotional support in return. What workaholics already possess, or what they have achieved so far, they often take for granted.

The art of appreciation is a skill that encourages contentment, and resists greed. Take pleasure in the beauty of the small, the ordinary, the mundane routines or special rituals – the precious everyday happenings of life.

The moment of truth lies in the present. Next time you find yourself struggling with some temptation, try standing still, wherever you may be. Listen to the rustle of the wind in the trees and feel its breeze, smell the rain, or hear its patter on the roof. Or sense the utter silence in the room. Is your heart beating too fast?

Do you really want to risk everything you now have? Is it worth it to cut corners, risk stealing something or cheating the taxman? Do you want to jeopardize your marriage by having a fling? Do you really want to drink or eat too much tonight?

Try to sort out your motivation *before* you act. Is it greed that is tempting you, or is it jealousy, envy, or some crazed ambition? Wisdom begins with awareness.

Be appreciative when something mysterious happens, as if by chance. A stranger approaches you at a moment of need, or you enter someone else's life at a crucial time. Without warning, your load is less heavy, or you've been enlightened in some way. In Jungian terms, synchronicity is a divine intervention acted through people and circumstances. A banker friend "just happens to call" when you've overspent and are contemplating "borrowing" some money out of petty cash. A self-help book catches your eye as you peruse the bookstore shelves. It offers specific advice that just might get you out of a jam you've created. "Did it jump off the shelf by accident?" you wonder.

- Is my humility intact?
- Do I neglect to fully appreciate what others do for me?
- Do I remember to verbally express my gratitude for others' generosity and reciprocate at a later date?
- Do I thank God daily for my blessings?
- Do I know how to ground myself when I'm faced with temptation?

Be fully present. There is no integrity in being only partly there! In *Care of the Soul* Thomas Moore describes a man who came to him deeply depressed. He seemed completely dissatisfied with his work. For ten years this man had planned his escape from a manufacturing-shop job. His performance suffered as he daydreamed of going back to school.

Moore asked him, "Have you ever thought ... of being where you are, of entering fully this job that you're putting your time and energy into?"

"A robot could do it better," the worker protested. "You're saying," he asked incredulously, "that I should go to this stupid job as if my heart were in it?"

Moore's reply was: "You're in it, aren't you?"

He comments further on the man's alienated and divided life: "The sheep of his work fantasies had been wandering everywhere but in the shop" (8).

Like this man, we must learn to find our way *through* our experiences by entering into our fate and emotions to taste our own life. Ask yourself:

- Am I emotionally there for those people who are significant to me?
- Do I listen carefully, and respond with honesty and respect?
- Do I make the people I know feel important and accepted?
- Do I consider myself trustworthy and compassionate?
- Am I fully present to meet my own emotional needs?

SOME FINAL THOUGHTS ON INTEGRITY

During the writing of this book, a persistent thought kept popping up: "Is it possible to possess integrity without compassion?"

I am left with no doubt about the answer to this question. Other-directed compassion and self-love are absolutely necessary and often our greatest challenge.

To have compassion, we must feel. In *Henry James: A Life*, Leon Edel quotes from a letter that James once wrote in reply to one from the daughter of his neighbour who had expressed her deep loneliness after her husband went off to the front: "I am incapable of telling you not to feel. Feel, *feel*, I say – feel for all you're worth, and even if it half kills you, for that is the only way to live ... to honour and celebrate these admirable beings who are our pride and our inspiration" (695). James found a new reason for existence, Edel writes, when he began visiting the wounded soldiers and victims of World War I. He came to the wounded not as a great writer but as a quiet, composed, kind, and warm presence who "conveyed almost in silent admiration without condescension, trust without question, an air of acceptance" (696). In other words, James showed unconditional love.

As Matthew Fox reminds us in *A Spirituality Named Compassion*, a genuine compassion reveals itself through acts of mercy, kindness, and justice. "Compassion leads to works. Feeding, clothing, sheltering, setting free, giving drink, visiting, burying, educating, counseling, admonishing, bearing wrongs, forgiving, comforting, praying" (8).

More than ever in our increasingly valueless society, we need spiritually wise role models to help us follow the Golden Rule of "Do unto others as you would have them do unto you."

Jean Vanier, the son of former Canadian governor general Georges Vanier, and founder of L'Arche, an international network of communities for people with intellectual disabilities, is such a man. In his book *Made for Happiness*, Jean Vanier describes his journey towards a compassionate "way of the heart." In 1964, he founded L'Arche and lived amongst and embraced individuals who could not participate in intellectual or abstract conversation but needed to have fun, laugh, and be loved unconditionally.

At the impressionably young age of thirteen, Vanier had joined the British naval school. As an officer he learned to be quick, competent, efficient and goal oriented but discovered that he needed to get back into his body and soul. After his departure from the navy, he sought to find the meaning of life in his Christian faith.

At the Catholic Institute in Paris in 1962, Vanier completed a doctoral thesis entitled "Happiness as Principle and End of Aristotelian Ethics," from which he drew the conclusion that Aristotle valued human beings for their rational and intellectual capacity alone. "With him there is no real compassion ... Aristotle could not conceive of the fact that weak people might be able to help a man to become more human, to grow in his humanity" (187).

Jean Vanier offers the sage advice that our lives and identity are shaped by the choices we make. If we choose to work for society and act for the good of others, he warns, "this implies that we choose the appropriate studies, that we accept guidance and have models, and that we engage progressively in political and social action in order to acquire experience; that we reject corruption, power at any price, and all forms of injustice" (151).

It seems fitting then to end with this truism: *Our choice to act with personal integrity does matter!* By keeping compassion front and centre in our own lives, we make the world a better place.

Integrity: A Personal Quiz

1 Do I have a healthy respect for rules, regulations, and laws?

2 Do I strive for humility and wisdom in my daily dealings?

3 Does compassion win out over critical judgment when I'm assessing a situation?

4 Do I actively "reality test" with others to avoid self-deception?

5 Do I avoid impulsive actions by building in a waiting period *before* I make a major decision?

6 Is my focus on "doing the right thing," rather than on whether or not I'll be caught if I don't?

7 Do I consider the impact of my behaviour on other people *before* I act?

8 Do I choose to tell the truth even when faced with the possibility of negative consequences?

9 Do I search for one of "life's lessons" whenever I inadvertently make a mistake?

10 Do I guard against laziness and sloth by being self-disciplined in *both* my personal and professional lives?

11 Do I consider the ethical and moral implications of my choices?

12 Is my conscience an effective monitor in critiquing my own thoughts and behaviours?

13 Am I fair and equitable in my dealings with others?

14 Do I accept that neglecting to tell the truth is a passive-aggressive form of lying?

15. Do I refrain from second-guessing others and ask them directly?

16 Do I consider it my duty and privilege to always act with integrity?

17 Do I express my gratitude to others who exercise their integrity with me?

18 Am I a responsible person when it comes to following through on a promise?

19 Do I try to understand others' actions even when I'm frustrated or angry with them?

20 Do I avoid projecting blame by taking 100 per cent responsibility for my own reactions to situations and people?

21 Do I consider perfectionism and idealism a distortion of reality?

22 Does my deeply felt compassion for others motivate me to take positive steps to help correct a wrong or injustice?

23 Am I reliable and reasonably consistent in carrying out my daily responsibilities?

24 Are my actions in harmony with my best intentions?

25 Do I counter my arrogant tendencies to feel special and superior by trying to be empathetic, to "walk in another person's moccasins"?

Bibliography

Ackroyd, P. *Blake*. Great Britain: Reed Books 1996.

Acton, Lord J. Letter to Bishop Mandell Creighton, 1877. In *Familiar Quotations,* edited by J. Bartlett, 663. 13th ed. Boston: Little Brown 1955.

Allen, B. "The Truth about Truth." *Toronto Globe and Mail,* 20 November 2004.

Bennett, L. "Still Captain Fantastic." *Vanity Fair,* November 1997.

Berglas, S. *The Success Syndrome: Hitting Bottom When You Reach the Top.* New York: Plenum Press 1986.

Blackham, H.J., ed. *Reality, Man and Existence: Essential Works of Existentialism.* New York: Bantam Books 1965.

Borowitz, A. *Who Moved My Soap: The CEO's Guide to Surviving in Prison.* Toronto: Simon & Schuster Canada 2003.

Boyd, M. *A Lover's Quarrel with the World.* Burlington, Ont.: Welch Publishing 1985.

Campbell, R. *Psychiatric Dictionary.* 5th ed. New York: Oxford University Press 1981.

Carter, S. *Integrity.* New York: Basic Books 1996.

Chesterton, G.K. (1908) "All Things Considered." In *Prophet of Orthodoxy: The Wisdom of G. K. Chesterton,* edited by R. Sparkes, 120. London: Harper Collins 1997.

Christian, W. *George Grant. A Biography.* Toronto: University of Toronto Press, 1993.

Clarkson, M., M. Deck, and R. Leblanc. *Codes of Ethics, Conduct and Practice.* Faculty of Management, University of Toronto. 1996.

Conrad, J. "A Familiar Preface." *A Personal Record.* 1912. Marlboro, Vt.: Marlboro Press 1982.

Corneau, G. *Absent Fathers, Lost Sons: The Search for Masculine Identity.*
   Boston: Shambhala 1991.

Cornford, F.M. Introduction to *The Republic of Plato.* New York: Oxford
   University Press 1945.

Curtis, C.P. *A Commonplace Book.* New York: Simon & Schuster 1957.

De Pree, M. *Leadership Is an Art.* New York: Dell 1989.

Dodson, J. *Final Rounds: A Father, a Son, the Golf Journey of a Lifetime.* New
   York: Bantam 1996.

Edel, L. *Henry James: A Life.* New York: Harper & Row 1985.

Festinger, L. "A Theory of Social Comparison Processes." *Human Relations*
   7 (1954): 117–40.

Fisher, R., and W. Ury. *Getting to Yes: Negotiating Agreement without Giving
   In.* New York: Penguin 1981.

Fox, M. *A Spirituality Named Compassion.* San Francisco: Harper & Row 1979.

Frye, N. *The Educated Imagination.* Concord, Ont.: Anansi 1993.

Gandhi, M. *Gandhi: An Autobiography.* Boston: Beacon Press 1993.

Gibb-Clark, M. "Attendants Fly Unfriendly Skies." *Toronto Globe and Mail,*
   28 January 1997.

Gladwell, Malcolm. *Blink: The Power of Thinking without Thinking.* New
   York: Little, Brown 2005.

Godin, S. *Wisdom, Inc.* New York: Harper Collins 1995.

Gostick, A., and D. Telford. *The Integrity Advantage.* Salt Lake City: Gibbs
   Smith 2003.

Guyer, P., ed. Introduction to *The Cambridge Companion to Kant.*
   Cambridge: Cambridge University Press 1992.

Halberstam, J. *Everyday Ethics.* New York: Penguin 1993.

Hart, A. *The Hidden Link between Adrenalin and Stress.* Dallas: Word
   Publishing 1991.

Havel, V. *The Art of the Impossible.* New York: Knopf 1997.

Hemingway, E. *The Garden of Eden.* New York: Scribner's 1986.

Hodson, N. "Lead Them Not into Temptation." *University of Western
   Ontario Business Quarterly.* London, Ont.: Richard Ivey School of
   Business, 1996.

Honderich, T., ed. *The Oxford Companion to Philosophy.* Oxford: Oxford
   University Press 1995.

Hotchkiss, Sandy. *Why Is It Always about You? Saving Yourself from the
   Narcissists in Your Life.* New York: Free Press 2002.

Hume, D. Essay, "An Enquiry Concerning Human Understanding."
   *Enquiries Concerning Human Understanding and Concerning the Principles of
   Morals.* 3rd ed. London: Oxford University Press 1975.

Ignatieff, M. *A Life of Isaiah Berlin*. Toronto: Penguin 1998.
– *The Rights Revolution*, Toronto: Anansi 2000.
Jenkins, A. "Person, Place, Thing." *Toronto Globe and Mail*, 22 March 1997.
Jung, C.G. *Psychological Types*. Princeton, N.J.: Princeton University Press 1971.
Kagan, J. "Personality Development." In *Foundations of Abnormal Psychology*, edited by P. London and D. Rosenhan. New York: Rinehart and Winston 1968.
Kennedy, J.F. *Profiles in Courage*. Harper & Row 1955.
Killinger, B. *Workaholics: The Respectable Addicts*. Toronto: Key Porter 1991.
– *The Balancing Act: Rediscovering Your Feelings*. Toronto: Key Porter 1995.
– "The Workaholic Breakdown Syndrome." In *Research Companion to Working Time and Work Addiction*, ed. R. Burke. Cheltenham, U.K.: Edward Elgar 2006.
Kirchhoff, H.J. "Joe Papp: Producer-Director's Failings Noted." *Toronto Globe and Mail*, 10 September 1994.
Krakauer, J. *Into Thin Air*. New York: Anchor 1998.
Krech, D., R. Crutchfield, and N. Livson. *Elements of Psychology*. 3rd ed. New York: Knopf 1974.
Lacey, L. "Leo in Love with Himself." *Toronto Globe and Mail*, 2 May 2003.
Lasch, C. *The Culture of Narcissism: American Life in an Age of Diminishing Expectations*. New York: Warner 1979.
Latane, B., and J. Rodin. "A Lady in Distress: Inhibiting Effects of Friends and Strangers on Bystander Intervention." *Journal of Experimental and Social Psychology* 5 (1969): 189–202.
Lloyd, M.P. *True to Life: Why Truth Matters*. Cambridge: MIT Press 2004.
Mandela, N. *Long Walk to Freedom*. Boston: Little, Brown 1994.
Menzies, H. *No Time: Stress and the Crisis of Modern Life*. Vancouver: Douglas & McIntyre 2005.
Miller, A. Foreword to *After the Fall*. New York: Bantam Books 1964.
Mitchell, A. "Hockey Coach Pleads Guilty to Sexual Assault Charges." *Toronto Globe and Mail*, 3 January 1997.
Moore, T. *Care of the Soul*. New York: Harper Collins 1992.
Murdoch, I. *Metaphysics as a Guide to Morals*. London: Penguin 1992.
Myers, I.B. *Manual: Myers-Briggs Type Indicator*. Palo Alto, Calif.: Consulting Psychologists Press 1980.
Nietzsche, F. *Beyond Good and Evil*. Introduction by M. Tanner. London: Penguin 1973.
Pascal, E. *Jung to Live By*. New York: Warner Books 1992.

Piaget, J. *The Moral Judgment of the Child*. 1932. New York: Free Press 1965.

Reik, T. *Listening with the Third Ear*. New York: Jove 1948.

RPS Courier System Co. advertisement, "If You Can't Teach the Old Dog New Tricks, Get a New Dog." *Time*, 9 December 1996.

Rumball, Donald. *Peter Munk: The Making of a Modern Tycoon*. Toronto: Stoddart 1996.

Saul, J.R. *The Unconscious Civilization*. Toronto: Anansi 1995.

Saunders, J. "Greed Was the Bait for FBI Stock Sting." *Toronto Globe and Mail*, 26 August 2002.

Scarf, M. *Intimate Partners: Patterns in Love and Marriage*. New York: Random House 1987.

Schachter, H. "Simplicity." *Toronto Globe and Mail*, 8 March 8, 1997.

Sharp, D. *Personality Types: Jung's Model of Typology*. Toronto: Inner City Books 1987.

Shelley, M. *Frankenstein*. London: Penguin 1992.

Shoalts, D. "Kennedy: There Are More Victims." *Toronto Globe and Mail*, 9 January 1997.

Smith, A. (1759) *The Theory of Moral Sentiment*, edited by D.D. Raphael and A.L. Macfie. Oxford: Clarendon Press 1976.

Sondheim, S., and J. Lapine. "Into the Woods." Original cast recording libretto. RCA Victor.

Stone, L.J., and J. Church. *Childhood and Adolescence*. New York: Random House 1968.

Subby, R., and J. Friel. *Co-Dependency: An Emerging Issue*. Hollywood, Fla.: Health Communications 1984.

Vaill, A. *Everybody Was So Young*. New York: Houghton Mifflin 1998.

Vanier, Jean. *Made for Happiness*. Toronto: Anansi 2001.

Waldie, P., and K. Howlett. "Reports Reveal Tight Grip of Ebbers on WorldCom." *Toronto Globe and Mail*, 11 June 2003.

Wilson, J.Q. *The Moral Sense*. New York: Free Press 1993.

Index